JUST IN CASE YOU WERE WONDERING

SHORT STORIES AND OTHER WRITINGS, FACT AND FICTION

WENDELL A. DUFFIELD

The opinions expressed in this manuscript are solely the opinions of the author and do not represent the opinions or thoughts of the publisher. The author has represented and warranted full ownership and/or legal right to publish all the materials in this book.

JUST IN CASE YOU WERE WONDERING
Short Stories and Other Writings, Fact and Fiction
All Rights Reserved.
Copyright © 2015 Wendell A. Duffield
v2.0

Photographs from Duffield Family archives
Sketches in "My Role in a Revolution" by Bronze Black
All other sketches by Kalynn Gunderson
Cover art and design by Eileen Westphal and Kalynn Gunderson

This book may not be reproduced, transmitted, or stored in whole or in part by any means, including graphic, electronic, or mechanical without the express written consent of the publisher except in the case of brief quotations embodied in critical articles and reviews.

Outskirts Press, Inc.
http://www.outskirtspress.com

ISBN: 978-1-4787-6385-7

Outskirts Press and the "OP" logo are trademarks belonging to Outskirts Press, Inc.

PRINTED IN THE UNITED STATES OF AMERICA

PREFACE

THE COLLECTED WRITINGS that comprise this book were completed over the course of a bit more than two decades, ending in 2015. They deal with a variety of topics, and report both fact and fiction, as explained where needed. These words probably would have stayed in the dustbin of my life had it not been for the suggestion of an enthusiastic friend who was familiar with some of the tales, and had in fact been a participant in a few of the described adventures. She is also an artist, and suggested that she illustrate some of the word pictures on a path to formal publication. Thank you, Eileen Westphal, for your confidence that publication was worthwhile.

Other than beginning the collection of tales with the story of my birth, the overall organization of the writings is rather random. A reader need not worry about using a bookmark to maintain a continuity of story flow. One may read a piece or two at one sitting, and later jump back in at pretty much a random page, without sacrificing time-line consistency. The logical bookends finale, of course, would be the description of my death. But that report would, to borrow from Mark Twain, be premature … as of 2015.

When fate unexpectedly directed Eileen to a new path, talented young artist Kalynn Gunderson filled the vacancy. I thank both Eileen and Kalynn for their contributions. They have helped make pages more interesting and entertaining than words alone can do. Any lingering shortcomings that lead to reader complaints should be directed to me. Compliments will be happily shared by all three contributors to the book.

OTHER BOOKS BY WENDELL A. DUFFIELD

Nonfiction:

    From Piglets to Prep School: Crossing a Chasm

    Chasing Lava: A Geologist's Adventures at the Hawaiian Volcano Observatory

    Volcanoes of Northern Arizona: Sleeping Giants of the Grand Canyon Region

    What's So Hot About Volcanoes?

Fiction:

    When Pele Stirs: A Volcanic Tale of Hawaii, Hemp, and High-Jinks

    Yucca Mountain Dirty Bomb

    Jiggles, Rolf, and the Remarkable Finale to Frank Stone's Career

CONTENTS

Getting Started 1
The Beginning of My Time 4
The Tale of a Tail
    A Short Story Richly Flavored with Fact 6
The Tale 10
My Harvard Education 34
Reflections on My Prep School Days, Fifty Years After Graduation 38
On the Occasion of Mother's Ninety-Fifth Birthday 41
My Dad: A Pioneer in Motorhome Design, Construction, and Use 42
The Orange Whale Goes Hillbilly 51
The Orange Whale Pulls a Wedgie 55
Dad Does It Again! 59
About Face and Full Throttle
    A Pilot's Chilling Tale 62
Picking a Career While Picking Rock 67
Thoughts On a PhD Thesis Proposal (Or)
    How I Almost Got Booted From Graduate School 70
Remembering Siemon "Si" Muller 74
A Spanish Lesson in Time
    Helped Me Translate a Macho Rhyme 76
Transition Time, Smoothed by Limerick Rhyme 80

~~Utterly Warm Memories~~
   Too Sappy
   ~~Utterly Warm Mammeries~~
   Maybe
   ~~Udderly Warm Memories~~
   Closer
   Udderly Warm Mammeries
   Yes! 82
Number Two Musings 88
Green Electricity from Sewage 96
Twice Bitten by March Madness 101
Pele: A Poem in Remembrance 106
A Funny Thing Happened at This Funeral 110
Parts of Speech 112
Organized Religion and Me 114
A Very Belated Confession and Apology 125
Limerick-Lubricated Transition Time Again 128
A Field-Work Adventure in Hawaii 129
My Role in a Revolution
   A Tale of Tectonic Shift 134
Serendipity and Science 140
Pickles 144
A Kilauea Lesson for Lovers 149
Kachina Justice 153
The Volcano That Wasn't: A Tale for Practitioners of Geologic
   Field Mapping ... and Other Thinking People 160
A Grand Time at Grand Falls 164
An Unforgettable Meet-The-Press Moment on the Alaskan
   Peninsula 166
Are The Headwaters Of The Mississippi River In South Dakota? 172
Changing Climate, The Keeling Curve, And Me
   Science In The Climate Change "Debate" 180
That Dammed Colorado River!! 185

GETTING STARTED

FOR REASONS THAT escape my aging memory today and may never be recovered during a tomorrow, from an inception at a youthful age I have enjoyed writing as a way to tell stories — perhaps in part to compensate for being a reticent conversationalist? The earliest physical proof of this on-paper communication penchant is a seven-page handwritten tale that describes my first lesson in piloting an airplane. The aircraft was a two-passenger tandem-seating Aeronca owned by Dad's farmer friend who hangered his escape from earthly toil at a long flat stretch of an alfalfa field. I think I was a fourteen-year-old lad at the time. That flight left me so excited and enthused (at age fifteen I got my license to legally pilot a small plane solo!) that I wrote the story as soon as I got home to a source of paper and pencil.

Mother tucked the resulting scrawled first-flight pages, along with other accumulating mementoes of my childhood, into a cardboard box that lived to become quite full in the attic of our two-story Victorian house in small-town Minnesota. She and Dad moved into a compact pre-fab home once all six of their offspring were adults living elsewhere. As a result of their downsizing, I inherited "the box" containing a non-organized olio of papers, photos, and other miscellaneous stuff related to my early years.

If I want to credit any outside motivator for my joy of writing, thanks must go in part to my mother. Besides giving birth to and raising six children, Mother taught in the hometown elementary school once we kids were a bit beyond diaper and nursing age. She very much appreciated the value of education and did her best to imbue that notion into her pupils. Here's an illustrative example of payoff for her efforts. A few years ago I accidentally reconnected with one of her grade-school students who has retired from a business career and now writes novels as the pastime of his autumn years. He emails me, and tells many others at his book-signing presentations, that his love of writing stems from an enthusiastic early teacher named Mrs. Duffield. I presumably soaked up much of what he did from that same inspirational person, though my classroom with her was at home rather than in the old tired and sagging clapboard building called Browns Valley, Minnesota, Public School.

Another of my early experiences that helped develop a love of writing came from the ninth-grade English teacher at that school. His name is Marlowe "Red" Severson — Red in reference to a thatch of colorful hair, which has since gone white. He began each class session by writing a topic sentence on the blackboard and then timing fifteen minutes during which each of us students had to write a pertinent essay. I wish "the box" Mother created for me had contained some of my efforts from that class, but … gone in the mists of time. Nonetheless, I vividly remember that Mr. Severson carefully critiqued our student writings. He offered no minimum-effort unexplained simple letter grades, typical of so many other teachers that I've had over the years of formal education. Instead, Severson returned our essays embossed with thoughtful suggestions for improvement and words of encouragement and praise where merited. The following sentiment may sound unbelievable, and I can't prove that it isn't, but I think I looked forward to the challenge of writing something legible, logical, and grammatical in those Monday through Friday English class sessions. In remembrance of his teaching style, decades after that ninth-grade class, I wrote a poem for Mr. Severson. I mailed him a copy of that verse. He returned it with a grade of A-minus. Whew!! But this time he added no helpful comments. Hmmmm.

I hope that at least some readers of this book will deem it worth the old Severson style of evaluation, with perhaps even an accompanying letter grade with a posted review. If you find what seems like unnecessary repetition of some details as you read through the book, please keep in mind that this is a compilation of writings created during a bit more than two decades; each piece is meant to be understandable on its own.

THE BEGINNING OF MY TIME

WE HUMANS HAVE "our time" on planet Earth. One is born, lives for a difficult-to-predict period of time, and dies. My time began on May 10, 1941, so all of my annual birthday ~~celebrations~~ recognitions have been on that calendar date. The older I get the less I feel like *celebrating* each event. That's too exhausting! As I type this note, it is May 9, 2014.

Mother's Day in the USA is the second Sunday of the month of May (a bit of unintended sing-song poetry there). Due to vagaries in the Julian calendar (and its slightly modified Gregorian version), the date for Mother's Day varies from year to year. In 1941, Mother's Day fell on May 11. When she was still among us, Mother liked to tell me the story of the timing of my birth. Here's her tale.

I went into labor on May 10. There was no doctor or hospital in our home town. [Browns Valley, Minnesota.] *I wasn't interested in another home birthing, so your Dad took me to the nearest place with proper facilities.* [Sisseton, South Dakota, about 12 miles west of our place.] *At the Tekakawitha Hospital there, Doctor Bates oversaw your birth. Late that evening, your restlessness told me you were ready to appear and enter the outside world. Doc Bates thought I might want to be able to say that I gave birth on Mother's Day, so he told me he could delay your appearance an hour or so until then. I knew that Mother's Day calendar date changes from year to year, so I told him I just wanted to get this over with. You were "officially" born at 11:30 PM on May 10, 1941.*

It's a fascinating story that I liked hearing Mother tell and retell. I think she was smart to not mess with the time when nature wanted me to appear. She'd already been through two birthings and would have three more after me.

Today is May 9, and as a Mother's copycat of sorts, I'm not waiting past one more midnight to recognize my birthday this year. I'm noting the passage of another year today, and will spend tomorrow trying to forget how old I am. My motto now is Carpe Diem, just in case the sun doesn't rise for me the following diem.

Meanwhile, for your possible entertainment here's a photo of me in the nude, taken not long after that 1941 pre-Mother's Day birthing event.

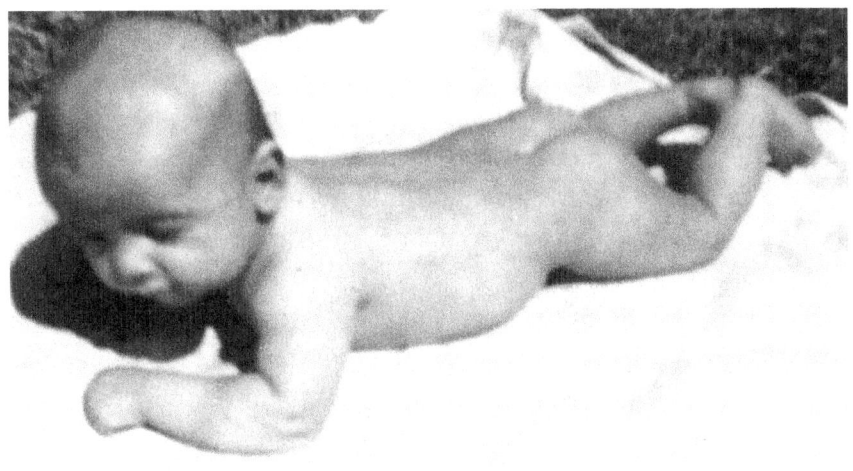

THE TALE OF A TAIL
A Short Story Richly Flavored with Fact

I include facts as accurately as I can remember them, several decades after the events occurred. I name myself Gene and my friend from a neighboring small Minnesota town I call Butch, false identities in deference to faded memories. But he and I were real boys who attended a certain New England Prep School. And love of the Cisco Kid TV program as an escape from academic pursuits there is authentic.

GREETINGS. MY NAME is Gene Peterson. I have a story to tell. I hope you'll read it. Won't take much of your time. You may find it entertaining, in part perhaps even entertainingly silly. Silliness or not, it's a tale whose theme should resonate with many readers. It's one from that coming-of-age genre, wherein two young teenage buddies struggle to cope with unexpected simultaneous mega changes in their lives. It's also the story of how their friendship grew stronger as they dealt with essentially new life styles — and how it has lasted beyond the teen years.

Friendships are good. Long-lasting ones are even better, if not the best. That's why I've recorded this tale. Even if few others fully appreciate the story, I know my pal-for-life Butch Anderson will, when I send him a copy. I should hurry to do so. We're both senior citizens now, and we all know what that can suddenly bring. I know what Butch will do when he gets to the line "Oh Pancho! Oh Cisco!" — if at that moment he is appropriately attired. Even now, I can picture a wide grin growing across his face as he zips into action. The story begins more than half a century ago — a once-upon-a-time setting.

As I look back that far from my current platform of age seventy-something, I see a contorted growing-up path created by unexpected turns of events, and accidents of the ilk that come without physical bodily harm — all tumbled in a tub of chaos. The unifying theme was *What will happen to me next?*

I have friends who tell me they knew what their life path would be from the single-digit years on. Some of these folks never strayed from that unidirectional track. It's as though these people went through life wearing blinders of the sort that keeps a team of work horses from being distracted by side issues. I had plenty of experiences with my Grandpa's horses to know about this situation. Well, good for my blindered friends, I guess. Even so, that may be safe but it's too predictable, potentially boring, and not my preference.

Maybe I was a kid whose unpredictable life path stemmed from a paucity of serious parental guidance. Oh, my folks tried, and pretty well succeeded, to teach me to be polite, understanding, etc. — to practice Christianity's version of the Golden Rule. But the only counsel of substance I can remember Dad offering as I aged toward becoming a professional adult was "Work for someone else, so you don't have the headaches that come with running your own business." Yes, he ran a business — a very small, yet time-consuming one. I can still visualize him at his desk at the end of each month, keying in numbers and then pulling the handle of a mechanical adding machine as he tried to balance the books. He hated that part of his business. It was not a good time for my siblings and me to be rollickingly noisy in the house.

At age seven, I declared my first-ever choice of a career path. I drove my parents to distraction by repeating ad nauseam, "When I grow up, I want to drive a road grader just like Bob Bynum does. When I grow up, I want to drive a road grader blah, blah, blah...." I was completely smitten by the thought of being in control of such a huge and powerful machine. I followed that man and his noisy yellow grader around our town just to see him push dirt and gravel — snow in the winter — into neat windrows and then spread it smoothly, or move it all to one side, or pile it, as the project required. Of course, my wish to be like Mr. Bynum was childish nonsense that never came to pass.

What *did* happen, though, seven years and as many different I-want-to-be mantras later was far beyond what I or anyone else in my family could have concocted, even if we had been under contract with a famous publishing house to write a fairy tale. In the form of a hand-written message on a post card, our household was visited by a surprise bolt of lightning with unimaginable power and implications for an inexperienced and sheltered family in an isolated Upper Midwest farming village of a few hundred people. That drab beige dog-eared piece of paper put me on a path that eventually led to a career whose name was an unknown word in our town. Talk about an unexpected jolt!

But first, I should mention the singular event in my life story that definitely was not an accident. It happened the evening that a nascent "I" went to a dance with Dad and came home with Mom. My birthday suggests that the event took place the night my parents attended the town's traditional fall celebration in recognition of a completed harvest and in preparation for another frigid Minnesota winter. I was literally a little squirt then. And the eventual result of that fruitful parental coupling would finally fulfill Dad's dream of having a son to carry on his family name. He was so utterly passionate about the future of his surname that he tried creating extra continuation insurance by fathering three more children after me. He finally gave up — or maybe Mom was too pooped to try again — when the result was three girls, added to the two others older than me. Dad would much later be tearfully disappointed in me for not carrying out his generational mission, even though I did follow his advice about a career spent working for someone else. My being a childless adult was yet another of my life's accidents, of the no-physical-bodily-harm variety. But I digress.

Meanwhile. Zap!! Back at age fourteen, I was separated from my family, my hometown, my friends, and all the comfortableness that goes with that kind of steady, nurturing, and predictable environment. Incredibly enough, the same thing happened to my friend Butch. The two of us were tossed into a new and strange world together. After a brief rocky start, we learned to cope — to cope quite well. And even though El Vaquero will never know it, the Cisco Kid helped us gain acceptance and a feeling of belonging in our new environment. The Kid spawned an inspiration for a rather bizarre ritual that strengthened our bond of boyhood friendship and that became widely popular in our new surroundings once word spread. I still practice that ritual, although the waning manual dexterity of septuagenarianism is taking its toll.

Do I have your interest? I hope so. Here we go.

THE TALE

"Boys will be boys, but at what age will they grow up?" From the lips of a seemingly exasperated Margaret Peterson, watching her forty-year-old son once again act the ten-year-old.

"THIS PLACE REALLY sucks," I said to Butch as we and a swarm of our schoolmates crept down icy concrete steps of the Thompson Gymnasium at Phillips Exeter Academy, into the dark of a moonless night. We zipped our jackets against the cold and pulled on woolen gloves. Being October, a taste of winter had arrived in earnest a bit early for Ivy League New England. The school's outdoor athletic events scheduled for earlier in the day had had to be cancelled.

"Yeah. You've got that right," Butch muttered. "It sucks harder than the vacuum pump Bickel uses in science lab. You can't tell by looking, but he claims that thing sucks all the air out of the big bell-shaped jar it's hooked to. If that's true, it's just like that thing they call rules at this school sucks all the fun out of being here." He looked around to be sure no faculty member was within hearing distance, and continued to complain at a lower volume to keep the conversation private. "What kind of place doesn't allow popcorn and cokes at a movie!! To say nothing about not being able to curl my arm around a date."

Butch and I were new preppies, geographically and socially at least a light-year from home, struggling to find a comfort zone in our new environment. We came from small neighboring towns in

Upper Midwest farm country, where the only ivy we knew of was the poison variety that was the bane of summer Scout camp up in the north woods. Many a Scout was known to find relief by squatting in the woods, only to suffer the pain and embarrassment of a swollen, tender, and itchy crotch and its attached male hardware for the next several days.

Neither of us had ever before been more than a day's drive from home. That was about two hundred miles, given the roads and cars of 1950s vintage. Now, nearly fifteen hundred highway miles from home, we were immersed in two centuries of New England traditions, which included the notion that true civilization in North America had not yet advanced westward beyond central Pennsylvania. At least that's the impression we developed from our first two months at the Academy. "It's like being in a foreign country," I wrote in a letter to my Dad. "One that has a superiority complex, too."

Butch and I had just watched a movie projected on the mottled and warped white wall of the basketball court — lousy substitute for a flat silver screen and a theater. The court's backboard partly overlapped the movie scenes. Music and dialogue echoed from gym walls like the wild cheers of basketball fans. Butt-aching discomfort inflicted by sitting on folding metal church-parlor chairs was right in character with the rest of the experience.

A Saturday night flick in the gym was the weekly Academy-approved entertainment for its students. Attendance wasn't required, but was strongly encouraged for educational values. Faculty chaperones made note of any regular absentees and nettled such a student in the classroom — unless a dorm Proctor reported that the absentee had stayed in his room to study, which brought words of praise. Butch and I had already figured out that nose-to-the-grindstone study was what the Academy was all about.

I gave him a gentle punch on the shoulder. "I'm so sick of the *in loco parentis* stuff this school throws at us," I said, mocking the Academy's adopted Latin phrase with a high-pitched nasal sound. "No to this. No to that. No to almost anything fun. We can't even go to the downtown theater where we could see Hollywood's newest."

"Amen!" Butch agreed. "And fancying up the rules with Latin

doesn't make 'em easier to take."

The town theater was strictly off limits. To be caught there would trigger immediate and automatic dismissal. The Academy described any fraternizing with townies and their way of life as unwise, if not socially undesirable. Though no perimeter wall existed, the Academy seemed physically isolated from the surrounding village. Everything the Academy needed to carry out its education mission was self-contained. The host town was superfluous, though occasionally the source of a few nuts and bolts for the physical plant — stuff that could be acquired at any commercial center.

In addition to discouraging interactions with townies, Academy professors were so relentless in their quest to waste no time in the education of their charges that they insisted on thought-provoking cinema to stress intellectual themes related to classroom subjects. Foreign films with English subtitles were a faculty favorite, selected to carry both language and life lessons. Appropriate French and Italian movies were regulars. Greek and Latin would have been top priority had they existed. Teen-pleasing oater flicks, cops-and-robbers adventures, and movies with more than a bit of exposed female skin were never offered.

Butch and I walked faster once off the steps, onto less slippery flat ground. Tonight's movie had been longer than the typical Saturday offering. Anyone not in his dormitory by ten o'clock would be locked out. When that happened, a dorm Proctor would notify the Dean who would send out a staffer to hunt down the unfortunate lad. Intentionally late or not, he would be sent home in the unforgivable disgrace of not measuring up to Academy standards. A victim of *in loco parentis*. For minor infractions of rules, the Academy might help the boy relocate to another private school that demanded less stringent standards of behavior — a prep school that would gladly take in just about any Academy reject. New England was replete with such institutions. Meanwhile a replacement for a student who was euphemistically "asked" to leave was a phone call away. A long prioritized list of candidates, whose parents anxiously awaited news of an open slot, added teeth to the threat of expulsion for rule breaking. Butch and I already knew of two schoolmates who had been so replaced.

Though the Academy's rules seemed unduly harsh, we toed the line, not wanting to disappoint our parents.

"Just think what we'd be doing tonight," I said wistfully "if we were back in the land of ten thousand lakes." I stopped and looked up into a cloudless sky to bond with home by mentally connecting the two outer stars of the Big Dipper with a line that projected to the North Star. I pointed. "There's the star of the state I wish I was in right now."

Butch's eyes followed my gaze. "Yeah. I wish I was home, too."

We exhaled long sighs. Our humid breath condensed into white clouds that dispersed into the surrounding darkness.

Like well-conditioned Pavlovian subjects, nearby schoolmates looked up where I was pointing, only to focus back toward the ground, with an audible "uuummm" from feeling duped rather than rewarded. "What are you fom boys up to now?" one asked. His pronunciation of *farm* identified him as a New Englander. Probably a Bostonian, I thought.

"We're just thinking about home," Butch said. "You can bet we'd be having a ball tonight if we were back in the land of *L'Etoile du Nord.*"

I watch as his pursed lips expelled an unsuccessful attempt at a French accent. Butch's recent introduction to that language hadn't done much yet to refine his Midwestern twang into a sophisticated continental sound.

"You eastern guys feel at home here cuz that's where you are. Gene and I feel like we're in a foreign country. We're still trying to figure out this weird place. The state says *Live Free or Die*. The Academy says live free and you're out of here. That's nothing like home."

I nodded agreement as Butch and I started walking again, gloved hands shoved in jacket pockets for added warmth. Students ahead and behind gathered into chattering mini cliques as they slogged toward dormitories to beat curfew time.

"Remember the car Dad bought me last summer?" I said, turning to Butch. A trip back home was taking shape in my imagination.

His "Sure do" came out with a sad and envy-tinged sigh. "What a cool machine. Wish I had a car like that. We had some good times in it before shipping off to this place." His tone-of-voice switched to hopeful. "Right before we left for the Academy, Dad promised he'd get me some wheels, if I make it through my first year here."

We moved shoulder-to-shoulder, following the outline of the snow-covered sidewalk. I walked duck-footed and dragged my feet to create parallel snow-free paths for a few strides, the way I did back home when my youngest sister followed me through a new blanket of the white stuff. Her short legs appreciated the help. I wished I was home with her and the rest of the family right now. Maybe driving my car in whirligig spinouts on a frozen lake. Or taking a run at a snow bank to see if I could plow all the way through. A shovel in the trunk would free me from any failed attempts.

"I love the alfalfa-green color of my rig. And there's not one scratch in that paint." I was sure from last summer's routine of applying Turtle Wax polish once a week.

"There's no scuffs on the white walls either," Butch said. "The fender skirts give a sports-car look." Nostalgic reminiscing triggered smiles.

"Boy, can that baby move in overdrive. With straight pipes barking like a machine gun!" I voiced the rise-and-fall rat-a-tat-tat-tat-tat noise created by revving and backing off the V-8 engine. A few nearby students looked toward the unusual noise and quickly focused back to their own conversations when they saw its source.

Butch remembered another sound. "I bet the radio's one of the best money can buy. It's like Buddy Holly and the Crickets are right there in the car with us." He broke into a few lines of *Peggy Sue* that were a lot more authentic than his go at French.

"Is that a moose mating call?" a winded schoolmate asked as he labored by. It was Bobo, a soft overweight kid from Massachusetts whose dorm was Barrett House. It seemed to Butch and me that too many of the eastern guys were overweight and out of shape. Not all of them, but a lot of them were. We were lean and manual-labor hardened, and figured there was no excuse for teens to be soft. The puffing Mass pudge had a long walk to get to his room before curfew.

"Yup," I agreed with Butch, ignoring Bobo. "I've got one hot forty-nine Merc! It only had fifty thousand miles when Dad bought it. That rig'll last me a long time."

"Okay. Picture this," Butch said. "It's one of those sum̄ nights that we just left behind." He grabbed my arm, edge of the sidewalk, closed his eyes, and relived t' — him sitting up front across the bench seat from mc "That's the one night farmers take a break from work. They put on their cleanest bib-overalls over a starched white shirt, load the wife and kids in the family car, and drive into town to shop and socialize." I was already nodding as Butch added, "You know what that means for us." We were both getting hyped up.

"I drive up to Wheaton to get you," I said, my eyes closed in concentration to help re-create the scene. "Then we head back to BV and start dragging Main." I held out my right hand shaped into a hollow ball facing downward, and twirled it in a wide counterclockwise arc as though starting a steering-knob spin into a U-turn while mentally caressing Marilyn Monroe, whose image decorated the knob. "Oooops! Sorry." My hand had smacked a passing schoolmate.

"Yeah. Dragging all four blocks of Main," Butch said through a chuckle. "Up and down. Up and down. Up and down. Enough to make a guy dizzy."

"Until ..." I boasted as I ran clumsy gloved fingers through my hair, "... until we pull up next to a couple of cute street-walking farmers' daughters and our good looks and lively conversation convince them to cruise with us."

Butch began his best seductive act of fingers through hair, and winked.

"We might even end the night with a park-and-purr session behind the county equipment shed." I paused to let that scene sink in. "And then we do the same thing the next Saturday in your town."

"Oooooh," Butch moaned. He pulled off a glove, shoved the hand deeply into his front pocket, and began to work a warm and instantly tumescent doink. "Change the subject, man. This is driving me nuts."

I knew what was happening. "Yeah. Okay. Okay. Back to reality."

Butch got his hand under control and gloved, and with another pair of sighs, we shuffled on and paused to scan for traffic at a street crossing. Some schoolmates were turning right, toward the nearby urt Street Market where they would buy the popular Saturday night sandwich called a grinder — wet-sponge soft from the juice of over-ripe tomato slices — and a quart bottle of super-carbonated saccharine orange soda to wash it down. This small family-run store was one barely-off-campus bit of towniedom not frowned on by the Academy. We students figured it was the Academy's way of admitting its dining room fare was less than tasty — especially Saturday's evening meal, which was always the same and about as popular as liver and onions.

"Hey Butch, Gene. You guys coming along to get some munchies? You must want something good after the yucky baked beans and black bread."

"Naw. You go ahead," Butch said. "That store doesn't carry the meat-and-potatoes kind of stuff we like."

We continued straight, into the dorm cluster of south campus. Back in my room, I had a box of Mom's homemade chocolate chip cookies, hidden as snacks to share with Butch. The grinder-and-orange-soda menu, rather than burger with fries and a coke, was as weird to us as the watery imitation malted milk the eastern kids called a frappe. The Court Street Market gang moved away.

"I know what you mean about going nuts," I said, when we were alone again. "We have to live like monks at this place. I used to think Dad and Mom have strict rules for me. But compared to *in loco parentis* here, I've got complete freedom at home." I glanced over a shoulder as though checking for an eavesdropper. "I wouldn't want my dad to hear me say that, though."

We walked past Wentworth Hall and then Amen, to the crunching sound of sticky snow compacting underfoot with each step. A leafless arthritic-looking network of ivy vines clung to the security-lit red brick walls of the dorms — another unmistakable reminder of how far we were from home. The only brick buildings back there were ivy-free banks and post offices. Schools were tired-looking white clapboard structures, typically in need of paint.

French Professor Thomas appeared from behind. At five-foot-eight, he was about the size of us teenage students. But his corrugated and weathered face topped by a tangle of gray hair reflected the advanced age typical of Academy faculty. Most of them were elderly

PhD-carrying academicians who had published several learned treatises since graduate school and who had written their own textbooks for use in Academy classrooms. Butch and I came from schools whose young teachers were fresh from limited college training that was more about how to teach than what to teach. They had teaching certificates, but not even a Bachelor's degree.

"Good evening Masters Peterson and Anderson," Thomas said in passing. He turned and backpedaled. We slowed to a near stop. "Did you enjoy the film tonight?"

"Yes sir," we answered disingenuously in unison. "It was real entertaining."

"And educational," Butch added.

"Good for you. I chose it to complement the lessons we're covering in the classroom. I hope you recognized that, Master Anderson."

"Yes, Dr. Thomas. I did," Butch said, figuratively biting his tongue, I was sure. He probably hadn't understood more than a few words of the film's dialogue. English subtitles that amounted to about one word for every ten spoken in French wouldn't help a beginner much with practicing this foreign language.

"*Tres bien*. Well boys, *a demaine*. Enjoy the rest of your evening." He pivoted and hurried toward home, having completed his Saturday night chaperone duties.

"What did he say?" I asked, once Thomas was out of earshot. I was taking Spanish as a required foreign language. That and Butch's French were our introductions to languages other than English.

"Good. See you tomorrow — I think. We'll be going to the Academy chapel service tomorrow morning, and he's always there."

"Oh yeah. Right."

Butch punctuated the chapel reminder with an "Amen." We picked up our pace. "Besides chapel, I wonder if our teachers ever take a break from their academic stuff. There's a lot more to the world than book learning. Like, why didn't Thomas say something about the World Series that's going on right now? And say it in plain English, not French. He knows we love sports."

I chuckled. "Well, if the Series came up we'd have to be careful not to let slip about Benno's betting pool. That guy takes a lot of chances. Talk about kids getting the boot if the Dean found out about Benno's gambling."

Gambling of any sort at the Academy, even of the penny variety over a hand of poker, was another *in loco parentis* trigger for being "asked" to leave. Back home, Dad and I regularly made bets during the Series and other big athletic events. Nickel and dime stuff that was fun and harmless. I had a dime riding on the Dodgers right now, leaving Dad with the Yanks. The winner would be able to afford an extra Snickers bar, which hardly seemed like a reason to kick a kid out of school.

"What do you think Thomas and his wife talk about at the dinner table — French grammar?"

"Yeah probably," Butch said, nodding his head. "In bed, too, I suppose."

"Back to the park-and-purr scene, huh." I watched as a sex-thought look started to cloud his eyes. "Hey! Keep your gloves on." I pinned his arms with a bear hug from behind. "We both wish there were girls at this school." I eased my hug.

"Well it ain't gonna happen. Boys-only is a New England prep-school tradition we're stuck with. But I don't understand why we can't at least have a female teacher or two. Instead of just a bunch of wrinkled old men who need lessons in how to smile and laugh."

"I guess if there weren't faculty wives on campus, we might forget what a skirt is."

"Maybe. But if we did, we'd remember real fast once we got home."

"Yeah! And Christmas break is less than two months away. We'll use my Merc for skirt chasing then!"

Our dorm was coming up on the left.

Hey reader, do you wonder what Butch and I were doing at the Academy if we were so unhappy with the place? Here's the short version of a longer story about one of my life's unpredictable unexpected accidents.

The Academy discovered us through a national search for

academically bright boys who could add diversity to an otherwise homogeneous elite New England student body. We had no knowledge about the search when it was underway. Then, surprise! What a surprise!! The Academy made contact via a plain brown two-cent post card. "Dear Gene Peterson," the message on my card began. "Would you be interested in attending our Academy?" And so on and so forth, the words extolling the many virtues of the place. My family had no inkling of what or where the school was. An encyclopedia entry filled in part of that void. I still remember Dad's exclamation of stunned surprise. "Gosh all fishhooks, Maggie! That place is a hundred years older than our town!!" Though confused by the card and its message, Dad and Mom were intrigued enough to search out more information about this mysterious school.

It happened pretty much the same way for the Anderson family.

Butch and I had to take a few tests to prove that our home-town academic records did in fact reflect intelligence. A few weeks later, following an interview with the Director of Scholarship Boys, the Academy offered full financial support. Proud parents agreed to send us east. The unrecognized, and soon-to-be-discovered unattractive part of the agreement was that the social, academic, and cultural shocks in store for two farm-country kids would be akin to plopping un-landed peasants into the daily life of England's monarchy.

Our trip back east was a muted adventure. Our parents couldn't afford the time or money to accompany us. Neither Butch nor I had travelled by train before. I enjoyed discovering new landscapes as they whizzed by out the window of the coach. But these several decades later I still remember the feeling of being lost and a little abandoned as we clickity-clacked over the rails from Minneapolis to Boston, and then on up to the Academy. I guess Butch felt like that, too. We hardly spoke the whole way.

Once there, we struggled to fit in. An Academy uniform of slacks, sport coat, white shirt and tie was required everywhere except on the athletic fields, in the shower, and in bed. So we unsophisticated lads had to buy new clothes and learn to weave the Windsor knot of a necktie. No more back-home blue jeans and tee shirts for every occasion but church, where ties weren't even a necessary part of the

Sunday dress-up costume.

The Academy's academic week started Monday morning and ended Saturday at noon. A daily diet of evening homework was necessary for us to keep up with the pace in the classroom. Academic standards were higher than Mount Everest, and a weak performance was sufficient cause for being "asked" to leave the Academy.

Back home, Butch and I had been accustomed to scoring straight-As without after-school homework. I think there were times when I even taught my teachers a few things they should have known. Ditto for Butch. Our notion of homework was mowing the lawn, raking leaves, shoveling snow, and the like — purely physical chores that our folks asked of us. Sometimes, we worked on our uncles' farms, too. Picking rocks out of corn fields, gathering hay bales into stacks for winter feeding, cleaning digested hay as cow poop from a barn floor, and such. We were mostly free to roam once those kinds of jobs were done. By contrast, The Academy's homework was brain strain, and the evening curfew/lights out smacked of a prison lockdown.

As a constant in-our-face reminder of the Academy's mission, HUC VENITE PUERI, UT VIRI SITIS, was carved large in stone at the center of campus — a promise to mold young boys into men. By the time we first arrived at the Academy, we'd already learned that Harvard men were the preferred product of that Latin exhortation. Only one hour north of the famous Cambridge campus, the Academy steered so many of its graduates onto a heavily traveled highway to Harvard that it created a near traffic jam.

Before the Academy intruded into our lives, Butch and I had never heard of Harvard — or any other college outside our home state. Saint Cloud State would have been my Harvard, if I'd been thinking about college. That place was close to home, and had one of the state's best coaches for basketball, my favorite sport. Butch once told me he'd go to Winona State if he went beyond high school, "because it's on the Mississippi." I think he harbored Huck Finn fantasies that came from reading a comic book version of Huck's adventures. Both of us eventually discovered even better "Harvards" far from New England.

All Academy students, physically coordinated or not, were required to participate in Saturday afternoon sports. This was the once-a-week chance for Butch and me to shut down the intellectual compartment of our minds and exercise the body. Raised on basketball, football, and baseball, we now learned about soccer, lacrosse and squash. But the rest of the Academy week, whose finale was the Saturday night movie, was about as far as one could stray from a life of easy-going public school, and whose Saturday night routine was hanging out with friends, dragging Main, and chasing skirts.

It was taking us real time, and some confusion, to get used to our new lives. A diet of huge and abrupt changes in food, clothes, study habits, living arrangements, the purported (imagined?) importance of a "distinguished" family history, sports, and even the sound of the English language was a challenge to stomach and digest. Though I never said so out loud (I'd been taught that teenage boys should control and internalize their emotions), I was homesick to the point of silently crying myself to sleep some nights. I think Butch was awfully homesick, too. But if so, like me, he kept that feeling to himself.

I moved off the sidewalk as we approached our dorm, and stooped down for ammunition. "Protect yourself, pal. I'm the guy who would have been BV High's ace pitcher if he'd stayed there." I scooped up snow, packed it, and threw — red maple leaves protruding from the missile. Early snow had beat out the ground crew's fall cleanup.

Butch ducked under the incoming snowball. We continued to target each other as fast as we could shape new ammo. A few dorm mates joined the fun.

The warning alarm sounded. "Cowboy time," Butch shouted. We dashed into Webster Hall for evening lock up.

We stomped sticky snow off our shoes in the entry vestibule and trotted down a central hallway to the ground-floor "butt" room for the weekly viewing of the Cisco Kid's adventures on the small screen of a black-and-white TV. Several other students were already there, anxious to enjoy authentic non-supervised Saturday night entertainment. There would be no purposeful language or life lessons, although a few new words of Spanish might pop up in the dialogue. Just the kind of raw fun teenagers deserve on a Saturday night. At least that's how

Butch and I viewed the Kid's adventures.

Each dorm at the Academy had a butt room. This was the one space where students were allowed to smoke and watch TV. Butch and I weren't smokers, but the TV was an unusual treat. Television hadn't yet reached our home towns. A few optimists had purchased sets, but the nearest program signal was broadcast from a small tower somewhere in the middle of North Dakota, providing a new type of Minnesota snow storm, even during summer heat waves. So when Butch and I saw a clear TV picture of Cisco Kid and his sidekick, we instantly bonded with their adventures.

Butch spun the channel-selection knob. A commercial for dog food was fading offscreen. Then the Cisco Kid and his partner Poncho appeared, astride their mounts.

"Here we go, *amigos*," I yelled, as a mesa-studded desert landscape appeared on the screen.

Two dorm mates, huddled in a corner, deep in conversation and smoking something called Gauloises, shouted. "Hey, cowboys, quiet down! We're trying to have a serious conversation."

"So go to your room."

"No! We think better while smoking. And you TV guys know the rules."

"Okay. Okay," Butch said, aware that to smoke in one's room was to invite being "asked" to leave The Academy. Expelled fellow students who had tried to hide that no-no had forgotten that a lingering tobacco odor soaked up by curtains and bedding was evidence as hard as a quarter-inch butt or two — in the Dean's system of justice, anyway.

At lowered volume, we watched acrobatic horseback riding, and bad guys being outdrawn in contests of six-shooter duels for the next half hour. During the final scene, we all joined the star and his partner in shrill congratulatory shouts of "Oh Pancho!" and "Oh Cisco!"

Then the reality hit that the Saturday night lights-out rule would soon be enforced. Our window to fun time was about to close for another week. And such a small window it was. The butt room emptied.

Butch and I climbed deeply worn oak stairs to the third floor. We topped out at the middle of a long central hallway. Up and down, a monotony of equally spaced doors and their transoms opened off the sides.

"See you tomorrow," I said as we exchanged shoulder punches. We had asked to be roommates. But the Academy's policy was to maximize cross-cultural exposure by pairing those of us from west of Pennsylvania with pure multi-generational New England stock. My roommate was a fourth-generation kid from New York. Butch's was from Boston. Nice guys, both, but different. There wasn't, yet, a lot of common ground to encourage conversation.

"Yeah. See you for chapel in the morning. Til then, I'm gonna dream about adventures in your Merc."

I nodded and raised my right hand, fisted with thumb up. We turned and shuffled down the hall in opposite directions.

I'm pretty sure we shared the same thoughts as we walked towards our rooms. Back home, we would stay up as late as the parents permitted. There was plenty of nighttime fun to be had. But here at the Academy, sleep — accompanied by pleasant dreams or simply blank-gray-matter unconsciousness — was a welcome, even an anticipated release from the nothing-but-business rigors of prep-school life. If you took away the Cisco Kid and sports time, from breakfast on I looked forward to the escape of being zonked in bed. Lights-out nighttime was the best part of each Academy day — hometown life tipped upside down. Butch and I didn't talk about it, but I'd have bet my Merc that he felt the same way. I guess this was another secret of the homesickness variety. Young men must retain a stiff upper lip, internalize emotional turmoil, and all that.

I stewed about this crazy situation during most of the sermon the next morning. But I did hear enough of the pastor's message to be reminded that it would be most ungrateful of me to not fully appreciate the excellent education provided by the Academy. I didn't doubt that that product would be delivered for students who lasted out their four Academy years. But I thought the pastor's message also ought to have mentioned that boys in their early teenage years should be allowed significant time for unmitigated fun. The adult decades would be plenty long for ultra-serious life, for things like making a living while raising a family. Naïve innocence would be lost soon enough. Meanwhile, I didn't see why it would be irresponsible or wasteful for teenagers to pursue play as well as book learning. I began to noodle that notion, and the vague outline of a plan to add fun to Academy life began to emerge — a kind of fun that I figured shouldn't arouse the *in loco parentis* patrollers unduly, even if they caught me in the act.

Another week began. Normal autumn weather reappeared. The snow melted. The grounds crew raked up the fallen fall leaves. A grizzled elderly farmer, who looked and smelled as though he hadn't shaved or changed clothes for a week or two, appeared on campus to sell the juice of his home-pressed apples from an oak barrel perched on the tailgate of a rusted pickup truck. Sales were brisk, until the Academy pronounced his product to be unsanitary. By Thursday he was banned from campus. It didn't matter that none of us students got sick from his apple-orchard treat. The Academy's application of *in loco parentis* thought we might. Another *in loco parentis* judgment sent two amateur chemists home from Wentworth Hall, when a Proctor discovered that they had added yeast to their juice, and gigglingly enjoyed the fermented result.

All week long, I practiced the extracurricular activity that I would soon unveil. I needed secrecy to polish my technique and to guarantee surprise when going public. The only privacy haven was a crapper stall in the shared restroom on third Webster. When the Proctor asked why I was spending so much time there, I flat-out lied that the cider had infected me with green-apple quickstep.

Saturday night rolled around. More beans and black bread. Another dull movie. Another exciting episode of the Cisco Kid. Another climb to the third floor, where escape from Academy life awaited in my sagging army-cot of a bed. Butch and I exchanged shoulder punches, said our goodnights, and headed down the hall in opposite directions.

At my door, I morphed into my version of a bad-guy. I contorted my face into an outlaw grimace, and swung around to glare down the hallway at the outline of Butch, who was about to disappear into his room.

"Hey! Come back here, you chicken-shit buzzard."

Butch backed into the hallway, surprised at the angry sound of a familiar voice. He turned and saw an ornery-looking friend. Confusion.

"What's up, Gene? Academy life finally too much?"

God yes, I thought as I worked to avoid smiling. "Listen you slimy slug. And listen real good. Get ready to slap leather if you hope to keep breathin'."

My hands hung open at my sides, next to a matched pair of imaginary holstered six shooters. I was a scurrilous outlaw calling out the Cisco Kid.

Still confused, Butch said, "Come on Gene. What's up?"

I bared clenched teeth, opened wide, curled my tongue into a slippery chute, and let fly a gob on the hallway floor. *I'll clean that up later.* A few seconds more and my right hand deftly unzipped the fly of my Academy standard slacks, reached inside, and extracted ...(No. No, not that you randy readers)... the long tail of my Academy standard starched white shirt. I pulled that cotton tail taut horizontally and aimed it at Butch.

"Kapow!! Gotcha man. Right in the gut. You need to work on your quick draw if you want to stay alive in this shit-eatin' world."

Now Butch understood. "Nice! Nice gun play cowboy. You're right. I need to practice my draw."

We shared a raucous laugh, followed by a loud "Oh Pancho! Oh Cisco!"

Up and down the hall, heads began to appear through partly opened doors.

"Quiet down you two!" Michael from Marblehead said. Benjamin from Boston joined in with a "Yeah!"

"Come on you guys. Get a life. It's Saturday night." I focused on Butch.

"Let's try another shootout. Only this time gentleman style so's not to upset our classmates too much." I motioned. "Meet me in the middle."

That was the head of the staircase, where we stood back-to-back.

"Twenty?" Butch asked.

"Yeah. Twenty."

We counted the paces before spinning, unzipping, drawing shirttails, and loudly faux firing. Butch slumped to the floor. I stood rigid as a stoic victorious nobleman.

"I hope that's more your style, Mike and Ben," I said. "More genteel."

Doors slammed, muting the sounds of *jeeze what clowns.*

"Hey. Screw 'em. This is fun," Butch said, as he stood. "Now the good old western way." We tucked shirttails, zipped flies and squared off at opposite ends of the hall. I challenged.

"Reach for it, you tub of guts. You're gonna be maggot meat by the time I'm through with you. Come on. Draw!"

Butch moved first. Following the faint screech of zippers, two white shirttails appeared almost simultaneously. He was already showing improvement.

Heads of more curious classmates emerged through partly opened doors along the hallway, only to disappear turtle-like as if avoiding the line of fire for real gunplay.

Shirttails and flies repositioned, we went at it again. It was Butch's challenge. A delay told me that he was frantically searching for the right words. Then ...

"I've had it with you, you slop slurpin' pig. Be a man and slap leather, or I'll walk down there and tear your arms out by the roots."

This time there seemed to be no winner. We were equal experts at a new sport. A few more quick draws, and we were ready to rest, amid smiles and giggles.

"This is the first night here that I'm not in a hurry to go to bed!"

"Ditto," Butch said.

"Thank you Cisco and Pancho!!" we shouted in unison.

I dragged the sole of a shoe across the splat of gob on the way back to my room.

Within a couple of weeks, the word and practice of shirttail quick draw, renamed QD, spread up and down the hall of third Webster. Then it seeped to the second and first floors and puddled in the butt room. And it began to show up elsewhere on campus. Earthy Benno compared the spread of the new sport to "The spread of bean-generated fart gas that fills the gym during a Saturday night movie." That breaking of wind was a popular student activity, one whose practitioners were many and impossible to single out for *in loco parentis* punishment. Saturday night beans were useful, if not tasty. Benno considered organizing post-movie QD contests — with him making book on the side, of course. But the risk of the dorm Proctor discovering the hanky-panky was too great, even for push-the-envelope Benno.

By the onset of Christmas vacation, the game's popularity was widespread among boys from west of Pennsylvania, as a harmless means of temporary escape from the academic grind. Our eastern schoolmates' capture by the fun factor evolved closer to the rate that Darwin might have imagined for his finches. It wouldn't peak until late in the academic year. By then QD found increasing traction, even with names like Rockefeller, Saltonstall, Irving, Benchley, Schlesinger — and with other famous-family schoolmates that I didn't yet recognize as such.

My family met Butch and me at the Great Northern Train Depot in Minneapolis. During the coming four years, the Peterson and Anderson parents would take turns meeting their Academy sons on school-break trips home. Limited free time and money dictated the shared duty.

My gut churned at seeing Dad, Mom, and my sisters, all smiling and waving wildly from the platform as the train screeched to a halt. The emotion of three months of accumulated homesickness rose in my throat, wanting release. But I successfully played the in-control-young-boy role, held back tears, and greeted them with muted monotonal hi's and tentative hugs. Dad slipped a dime into my hand, saying "Here's your Series winnings."

Butch watched closely. I think he expected me to break down. He probably was relieved that he wouldn't face the same test of his "manhood" until we had deposited him at Wheaton.

Luggage in the trunk, nine bodies wedged into Dad's '53 Pontiac, and we headed west to BV, dropping Butch off along the way.

I quickly got into the swing of holiday parties with my old hometown friends. Butch and I did our Saturday night cruising in my Merc. All too soon it was time to ride the rails back east.

The Academy schedule and grind were unchanged. But the temporary escape provided by QD was now widely and regularly practiced. We had to avoid detection by professors, proctors, and most especially Herr Kessler, the always-frowning Academy Dean, whose rigid interpretation and strict enforcement of *in loco parentis* was rumored to stem from Germanic roots.

The places we played! Dorm hallways and butt rooms were the safest, and therefore the most common settings. As our courage (or was it recklessness?) grew, QD face-offs migrated to campus pathways and eventually to the sacred central Academy Quadrangle, though only after thorough scouting for possible adult observers.

Creative Benno introduced QD to the classroom! The Academy's Harkness Plan limited class size to a dozen students and required seating around an oval table. The professor sat at one of the tight-curve ends. For us students, there could be no hiding in the back row. But there was ample hiding of a body below the waist, under the table. Two students would agree to a classroom QD contest ahead of time. They sat on opposite sides of the oval. Quick Draw was triggered by any one of a variety of signals. Perhaps a third-party cough, a throat clearing, or a pencil tap. It was impossible to see who won, and unzipping while in a seated posture was awkward. But the excitement of playing QD in the sacred Harkness setting was reward enough. I suppose Edward Harkness, the benefactor who made the small class size affordable, would be mortified unless, unlike Herr Kessler, he had a sense of humor.

Robes provided even better cover than the overhang of a Harkness tabletop for surreptitious QD. As one sleeve hung armless, QD practitioners who were members of the Academy's chapel choir (including yours truly beginning with year two) were able to hone their technique while singing the purported virtues of organized religion. Similarly, a number of veiled QDs occurred under the cover of robes at graduation.

By the end of that first Academy year, a new student tradition had been established. A new New England tradition, and quite unusual for the Ivy League! As co-inventors, Butch and I garnered some fame and respect from schoolmates. We wondered what the Academy's founder would have thought about QD at his otherwise stolid institution.

In following years, initiation of incoming preppies included indoctrination into the finer points of calling out a QD contest, with the understanding that a first-year student would never outdraw an upper classman. QD even impacted the business of George and Phillips Haberdashery, the Academy-approved local clothing store where students bought Academy uniforms and other Ivy League attire. The demand for slacks with the once popular button-style flies plummeted.

The accumulation of exploits to flesh out my tale might well have screeched to a halt when grades were reported at the end of my first year. One B, three Cs and a big fat D. My days of scoring straight As were distant history, never to be repeated. By my parents' award formula, (a dime for an A, a nickel for a B, nothing for a C, I owe them a nickel for a D) I deserved zero, rather than the usual fifty cents I regularly earned back in BV. Discouraging! And would Academy elders judge me to be a failure?

The Director of Admissions called me to his office. He stared down at me through bottle-thick eye glasses and said, "Your academic performance to date has been a bit marginal, son." I interpreted the following pause as an unspoken *you're out of here*. Then, incredibly, he added "But we want you to return for year two. We must see improvement next year. Don't disappoint us." I nodded my yes and exited in silence.

Right after that stunning surprise, the Director of Scholarship Boys summoned me. He was a short stout man, with a bald pate as nearly spherical as I've ever seen on a human body. He always wore a smile, which seemed appropriate for someone whose task it was to dole out scholarship money, a commodity not in short supply at the Academy. But today I wondered about that smile. *Oh oh*, I thought. *The Academy is willing to take me back, but only without a scholarship. There's no way my family can afford the tuition.* Instead, Hammy's message was "Starting next fall, my budget will pay for air travel back and forth between Boston and Minneapolis. That's in addition to your regular full scholarship."

I must have looked agog with disbelief! "Are you okay, son?" he asked. Before I could answer he added, "When you come back next fall, go to George and Phillips and get some proper Ivy League clothes. A corduroy sport jacket with leather elbow patches. That sort of thing. If you're going to be with us for the duration, we'd like you to look like one of us. Just sign for the clothes. The bill will be sent to me."

"Yes sir," I said. I didn't understand the Academy's award formula, but I sure preferred it to the one back home.

Butch had a similar story to tell.

Three years later, Butch and I graduated in the top quarter of our class. We each did a victory QD beneath the robe, while accepting a diploma with the free hand! We had developed efficient study habits, toughed out the Academy grind, lived up to Academy standards, and somehow avoided becoming victims of *in loco parentis*. Transformations along the way were remarkable. Shortly after the first-year Christmas break, feelings of homesickness disappeared. Yes, I still missed my family and home-town friends. But there was no more crying myself to sleep at night. And I no longer visited the Academy Post Office, daily, in hopes of another letter from home. As days stretched into months and eventually into four years, Butch and I discovered that teen-aged boys of diverse backgrounds share enough values and desires for a friendly coexistence, even if not as buddies figuratively joined at the hip.

Still, we remained suspect and somehow flawed in the eyes of some rigidly traditional New Englanders. Here's an extreme example. During senior year, my English professor always addressed me as a *Midwestern clod*. He also gave me the second D of my Academy record. Maybe I deserved the D, though I don't think so. The *clod* calling was harder to swallow. That professor addressed my Harkness Table classmates by their names. Maybe he thought his use of *clod* for me was appropriate, but my amateur character analysis was that he was sick, if not purposefully mean. I internalized festering feelings about him throughout that year. I wanted to tell him to shut up, but ... I feared that the broad reach of *in loco parentis* might victimize me. By then I had far more invested in the Academy than I was willing to risk losing. So it was always my polite *yes sir* to him, in response to his *Midwestern clod* at me. Well, this so-called clod and his best friend from far far west of Pennsylvania graduated with honor from The Academy. And now I can safely say, "Stuff that up your over-sized hairy proboscis and choke on it, Professor H. Darcey Curwen ... you pompous crusty arrogant supercilious arse." It feels good to write that.

Diplomas in hand, Butch and I said goodbye to the ranks of PUERI, joined the club of VIRI, and moved on to college. Four years in the New England preppie environment gave us an excellent high-school education. It also convinced us that we were not of the Ivy League ilk. We would not travel down the busy highway that led from the Academy to Harvard. Instead, we headed toward home terrain for undergraduate degrees. Four years later, we were all the way to the Pacific Coast for PhDs, Butch at the University of Oregon and me at Stanford.

The final chapter of this tale (or is it the penultimate, since Butch and I are both still breathing and mobile?) is about the role QD plays in maintaining our friendship. Geographic separation and the passage of time test that bond. As a geologist, I chase volcanoes here and there around the globe while Professor Butch probes the secrets of chemistry in his hi-tech university lab. A few letters and phone calls, and now emails, all punctuated with "Oh Pancho! Oh Cisco!" have helped keep the friendship actively intact. We wonder whether QD is still practiced at The Academy. We think not. The place went coed eleven years after we graduated, a change that might have been the death knell of our quick draw game — at least for the XX-chromosome carrying part of the new student-body mix. We suspect that other fun diversions of a coed variety are now in vogue — teens being teens.

My wife thinks QD is silly, but still loves me. My mother often wondered aloud about my mental age, too, whenever I demonstrated my QD prowess for her. But her smile, when the shirttail appeared, belied any true disapproval. I was never sure how Dad felt about my attachment to QD into adulthood. He lost a lot of interest in me four decades ago, when I subjected my vasa deferentia to the scalpel, cutting off the means of passing his genes and name on to the next generation. Sadly, we parted with unresolved differences about some of life's important issues. But the QD game has always buoyed my spirits. Everyone should have a QD or its equivalent. Life without some QD-style fun is life without enough fun. Arthritis permitting, I will practice QD to the end.

At that end, my epitaph can say "He died with his boots on and with a starched white shirttail firmly in hand." Wouldn't that scene make for interesting open-casket viewing! Somewhere, Butch would smile. And the aura of the Cisco Kid would permeate the environment.

MY HARVARD EDUCATION

HARVARD UNIVERSITY WAS established in the colony of Massachusetts during the year 1636. This was the first institution of higher learning within a geography that would eventually become part of the USA. From its early beginnings, Harvard was described as the crème-de-la-crème of Ivy League Universities, and today is recognized nation- if not worldwide as superlative in far too many higher-education categories to enumerate here.

And so it was that when I, a pre-college student attending nearby Phillips Exeter Academy in New Hampshire, was invited to visit this vaunted institution, my enthusiastic acceptance was a no-brainer. Who wouldn't want to rub elbows with the best!?

The year was 1958. I was what Exeter calls an Upper Middler — a high-school junior in common-language parlance. I had arrived at Exeter, quite unexpectedly, as a small-town Minnesota farm boy uprooted from rocky cornfield country and replanted into richly intellectual New-England turf.

My invitation to visit Harvard came from Exeter schoolmate Stephen Schlesinger, who was one of a dozen of us prep-school boys who occupied a small dormitory called Barrett House. The time was a spring break (Easter?) from our intensive academic regimen. Steve's father taught at Harvard. Little did I appreciate then how famous Arthur M. Schlesinger Jr. already was and would increase to be even more so throughout the coming of the John F. Kennedy Presidential years and beyond.

Our south-bound train ride to Cambridge took about an hour. Steve and I shared his room in the Schlesinger home. I was introduced to the family, including, if memory serves me well, a grandmother or someone of that age group, with Minnesota roots in her youth. In hindsight, a Minnesota connection may have been part of the reason Steve invited me to visit his home. Minnesotans can be hard to find in New England! And they do enjoy reconnecting with each other when separated so far from their low-keyed and comfortable home base.

The event of my Schlesinger visit that I remember most vividly was a dance organized for Harvard-faculty children of high school age. Phillips Exeter Academy was an entirely male institution until 1970. The prospect of this 1958 Exonian socializing with a bevy of teenaged females was quite a hormone stimulant!

Memories of the day, climaxing in that dance: At home, Arthur M. Schlesinger Jr. kept a within-reach bottle of whiskey around the house as he paced, read, and jotted notes — taking an occasional sip of liquid to stimulate and lubricate the muse, perhaps. During a family auto tour to show me the Harvard campus and surroundings, Schlesinger kept a book in hand, which he read at intersections while waiting for the red semaphore to go dark as green was illuminated. A family member had to remind him of the color change in order to avoid horns blaring from behind in cars loaded with impatient occupants.

At some point that afternoon, we visited a clothing store where I rented a tuxedo. The dance would be quite formal. And a few hours later, there we were — Steve and I mingling with scores of lovely gown-clad age contemporaries. He knew most, and I knew none.

I've never been a natural dancer. In fact, I've never truly enjoyed dancing, even after some training. But that evening was different, for the obvious aforementioned gender reason. I thrilled to the female touch and fragrance as I barely avoided stepping on the toes of a dozen and more dance partners that night.

Witty conversation, rather than awkward feet, was my notable stumbling block. Because summer vacation was only weeks away, once names and other introductory info had been exchanged between me (the Minnesota stranger) and the Harvard faculty girl in my arms, her talk drifted to *What I will be doing this summer.*

All of my dance partners rhapsodized about plans to again tour parts of England, France, Italy, or Spain or perhaps all of Western Europe. I had never been abroad. My only foreign foray to date was a drive from Minnesota barely into Canada so our family could boast back in the hometown that we had been outside the USA. Ergo, when a dance-partner's silence invited my description of summer plans, I simply replied "I'll be spending time at home with my family."

I knew this meant manual labor on my uncles' farms and at my dad's Sinclair gas station. But I (perhaps foolishly?) felt embarrassed to go into those details. Instead, I gently prompted my dance partners to tell me more about Europe. I listened, and I absorbed like the proverbial dry sponge. Though I didn't fully realize so then, I ended that remarkable evening with an indelible mental outline and primer of what my future should be.

After Exeter, I left the heady aura of the Ivy League terrain for the relative security of feeling at home in the Upper Midwest for an undergraduate college education at Carleton College. Classmates there chided me when I selected geology as a major, their mantra being that one should major with a pre-med or pre-law emphasis, or otherwise be prepared to live as a relative pauper later in life. But, I reasoned, doctors and lawyers and such tend to stay in one country and state or city, anathema to my "Harvard Education" lesson. So geology it was — all the way to a PhD from Stanford, which is sometimes called the Harvard of the West.

During the following forty years devoted to studying and writing about volcanoes, my field projects took me to volcanic archipelagos of the Atlantic, Pacific, and Indian Oceans — and to land-bound volcanic terrains on all of Earth's continents, save Antarctica. Only aging tired knees keep me from making that one remaining venture. Mount Erebus there is uniquely famous for a lake of roiling molten lava that contains gobs of platy feldspar crystals up to several inches long. Nonetheless, I can still revel in memories of so many cultures and landscapes and cuisines and languages sampled on the job! I thank my "Harvard Education" for prompting me to pursue this rewarding career path. Not all rewards are measured by dollar signs and material things.

Meanwhile, and flavored with a bit or irony, many of my now-retired undergraduate classmates who chose stay-at-home high-paying careers are discovering that with free time for world travels, their knees (as a metaphor, if not the actual cause) keep them from the joys of experiencing so many of the wonders of distant lands and peoples.

And the moral of this story is … Well, I leave that up to you.

REFLECTIONS ON MY PREP SCHOOL DAYS, FIFTY YEARS AFTER GRADUATION

THE MOST RECENT information about plans for our fiftieth class reunion arrived in my snail mail today (November 20, 2008). Hearty thanks, to whomever, for the cute mouse pad and for the class of 1959 website address. But darn, my excitement ebbed when I visited that site only to discover that I'm still a non-entity for Exeter. There is someone listed by the name of Wendall Duffield, though ... close enough to my real name that I'll just assume Wendall's identity and participate in the reunion plans. The following is my contribution for the booklet that will be published.

I'm one of the "farm kids" recruited by Exeter's Director of Scholarship Boys, Hammy Bissell. He came all the way to Minnesota to interview me, and that meeting led to my joining the Academy's ranks for the class of '59. If you're interested in the longer version of my recruitment tale, read *"From Piglets to Prep School: Crossing a Chasm."* As the book title suggests, my life at Exeter was a far cry from that in a really, really small Minnesota town.

Fact is, I was not a particularly happy person at the Academy. The highlights of the place for me were athletics and, believe it or not, sleeping. Something I invented and named Quick Draw also helped pass the otherwise incredibly slow passage of Academy time. One of several lowlights was the lack of coeds. But the lowest of the lowlights was having Instructor H. Darcy Curwen regularly call me a "Midwestern Clod" in his English class during my senior year, rather than Wendell, or even Wendall. At graduation, I (foolishly?) asked him to write in my PEAN yearbook, and his penned parting thought was "I really hope you'll carry the great light out into the darkness." He was quite disappointed that I was not going to stay east for a college education in his superior Ivy League.

But hey, I made it through the PEA grind, went on to college at Carleton in Minnesota, then to Stanford for graduate school, and now fifty years later can say that Exeter is not such a bad memory anymore. A bit ironically, my entire post-Exeter education/career path has been a rocky one, literally; I became a geologist who specializes in studying the solid products of lava erupted by volcanoes. My employer of thirty-two years, the U.S. Geological Survey, assigned me to projects all around the globe, providing so much international travel that now, in retirement, I prefer to stay in the USA. I "retired" from the USGS in 1997, at Flagstaff AZ, and immediately moved across town to become an Adjunct Professor of Geology at Northern Arizona University. Interacting with students at NAU makes me feel younger than I am. And as long as my legs held out, I kept climbing volcanoes to learn more of their secrets.

In "retirement" I've discovered that I enjoy writing for a broad readership, rather than only for a bunch of pointy-headed PhDs who mostly read the results of their colleagues' research projects. To date, I've managed to get six popular books into print and several shorter pieces in magazines and newspapers. I'm sure that H. Darcy Curwen would judge that none of my writing is great literature, but I enjoy the process, and it's something I can do when too tired to scale another volcano.

I met the love of my life, Anne Woodhams, at Carleton. We're now into our forty-fifth year of marriage. As youngsters with raging hormones, we had planned to start a family once the PhD was in hand. But during my grad-school years at Stanford, Anne worked for a biology professor by the name of Paul Ehrlich. Our family plans went the way of the dodo when Paul established an organization called "Zero Population Growth." Our time for children has been, and remains, fulfilled by the umpteen nieces and nephews of our seven siblings.

I regret that I haven't stayed in touch with Exeter classmates and friends since graduation. But then the lack of contact has been a two-way street. I see the name of my roommate of three years in the website class roster, but even Dave and I have not been in touch for the past fifty years. A few months ago, in a fit of nostalgia, I made email contact with Barrett House schoolmate Stephen Schlesinger, having read one of his blog postings. Steve kindly answered my message, including the fact that he had no memory of who I am. During my Upper Middle year I spent a long holiday weekend with the Arthur Schlesinger Jr. family in Cambridge at Steve's invitation, an experience *I'll* never forget.

But that was then and this is now. It's five pm ... time to leave my NAU office and go home to my dear Anne where I'll mix a Cuba Libre for tasty sipping as I reconnect with Exeter by reading a few essays from the 1965 *Exeter Remembered*. Attending Exeter certainly changed the trajectory of my life. But whether that change improved what my life would otherwise have been will never be known. Though my ambivalence is palpable, I generally prefer the down-home life of Lake Wobegon to that of Ivied Cambridge or New Haven.

I wish all my Exeter classmates a fun and successful reunion. I don't anticipate making the trip. But I'd enjoy a visit if some of you get to Flagstaff.

ON THE OCCASION OF MOTHER'S NINETY-FIFTH BIRTHDAY

A woman I know watches over my life.
Some seem to think she's just my father's wife.
But she is much more than a wife to a man.
She is an angel with two helping hands.

She's kept me fed … tucked me into bed.
She's kept me in clothes … wiped my runny nose.
She's soothed my tears … chased away baseless fears.

If love is defined as helping another,
Then love's quintessence is my dear sweet mother.

MY DAD: A PIONEER IN MOTORHOME DESIGN, CONSTRUCTION, AND USE

IN 2000, MY wife Anne and I made a purchase that neither we nor the friends who know us best would ever have anticipated. We bought a brand-spanking-new motorhome. In our "younger" years we were members of a subpopulation that sometimes scoffed at such machines as gas-guzzling road hogs, especially when our little VW was buffeted by the wind gust of a passing motorhome. But with the broader perspective that comes with age and in recognition of the facts that I recently retired and that we want to begin to see America from ground level rather than from thirty-five thousand feet through the window of a jet aircraft, we joined that rapidly growing gregarious group of motorhome owners.

An added pleasantry that has come with having our motorhome, and the fundamental motivation for writing this story, is the rekindling of memories of a motorhome that my dad designed and built, way before the commercial dandies of today were a reality. He was truly a pioneer in motorhome design and construction, but our family was unaware of and probably didn't even care about such status at the time. Dad was always tinkering and building things, and the motorhome was just another of his projects.

Dad and Mother raised their family of six children (five daughters and me) in Browns Valley, Minnesota, a town of almost a thousand inhabitants within rock-throwing distance of South Dakota. Though my parents always provided us kids with perfectly adequate food, shelter, and clothing, the trinity of necessities for "modern" living, family vacations were at the ragged edge of affordability. Staying in hotels was out of the question, and besides, no conventional automobile could comfortably accommodate two adults and six squirmy young kids for hundreds of miles of highway travel between hotels or other destinations. Nonetheless, my parents wanted family vacations as part of our growing-up experience, so Dad created one of his typically functional though less-than-beautiful solutions to what seemed an intractable space/money problem.

The solution came in the form of a retired school bus whose general appearance suggested an inability at mobility. The time was 1949, although the bus was already several years old by then. The body (by Blue Bird? Carpenter?) was of forty-eight passenger capacity, which meant twelve, two-student bench seats on each side of a central aisle, and the chassis was by General Motors Corporation. An inadequate-looking six-cylinder engine supplied dual rear wheels with what little power it could muster through a standard transmission with four forward gears.

The body tint was the severely sun-bleached yellowish orange typical of most old school buses. During the years of carrying students, the left rear springs had lost more of their rebound than those on the right (all the heavy kids sat on one side?), imparting a noticeable list to the hind quarters of this long orange beast. Moreover, when left to its own factory-supplied means of support, each front fender sagged to the point of nearly rubbing the tire beneath. The previous owner of the bus had addressed this unacceptable means of accelerated tread wear with silver-colored metal straps, one for each fender and each about four feet long by two inches wide, bolted to the fender on one end and the bus body near the windshield at the other end. Unfortunately, the fender lifts had not been applied equally, resulting in a right fender noticeably lower than the left one. Thus, in combination with a saggy left rear the bus appeared well on the way to the twisting spiral shape of a helix … or that of a gleefully surfacing whale.

The name of the school that the bus once served had been removed, perhaps to avoid any embarrassment that might come from association with such a tired and faded relic. However the engine apparently was reliable, and the body, though certainly not attractive, seemed sturdy enough to provide many more miles of safe road travel. So Dad bought this machine, almost certainly after some seriously animated negotiating, and drove it home where his version of a school-bus conversion to motorhome could get underway. During the following several weeks of his spare time, Dad designed and built the entire new interior of the bus, with minor help from us kids when that was possible.

First, those twenty-four seats had to be removed. They were simply bolted to the floor, and we kids took delight in removing the bolts as an exercise in permitted, in fact requested destruction. Dad reused most of the bolts to help build and then attach furnishings into the nascent house on wheels. Two of the benches were repositioned and used for seating at a dining table. Not being one to waste perfectly good materials, I suspect that he later found a use for the rest of the seats, or perhaps he traded them for the parts needed for what was about to take shape in our orange whale.

From back to front, the left side of the reconfigured floor plan included a toilet stool, bunk bed, cooking stove, and dining table with the two bench seats mentioned above. The table could be collapsed and the front bench turned on a swivel to provide forward-looking seating for us while underway. The right side included a storage closet, bunk bed, icebox, and roll-away bed that was folded and strapped to the wall while underway. Mother and Dad used the roll-away bed. My two older sisters and I each had our own bunk, while my three younger sisters were stacked head-to-toe-to-head in one bunk, in recognition of the typically tapered shape of the human body.

Air-conditioning was provided by opening any or all of the twelve side windows, one for each adjacent pair of the original bench seats, and heating was supplied by an adequate selection of clothing and blankets.

To accommodate a ten-gallon propane bottle that powered the cooking stove, Dad built a "back porch" by bolting a three-by-six-foot platform to the bus's frame. The back porch also provided space and support for three five-gallon jeep cans that held a gasoline reserve for the bus's engine. The back door of the bus opened onto the porch, which was a convenient escape hatch when the playfulness of us kids called for one. The back porch was also where dishwashing and Dad's ritual morning shave took place.

Left to right: Happy(?) campers Mary, Jackie, and Jean standing on the back porch.

Drinking water was carried in a couple of five-gallon plastic jugs, gray water went right out the door or through a drain hole in the floor, and black water (is the EPA listening?) was sometimes deposited in the ditches of remote rural areas. The proper dump stations of today simply did not exist back then. Our toilet was nothing more than a piece of (sanded!!) plywood with circular cutout, mounted over a five-gallon metal bucket. Next to the roll of toilet paper sat a small can containing lime that was used to dust any offerings. In fairness to Dad's planning and our attempts to respect health standards, we used the toilet only in rare emergencies. Otherwise, we became well acquainted with the many public facilities at parks and gas stations. These usually also served as our dump stations.

Night light was provided by flashlights and a couple of six-volt bulbs, mounted on the ceiling of the bus and powered by the bus's battery. We had to restrict the use of these lights, since there were no backup batteries and certainly not a built-in generator.

Without such a generator and lacking propane-powered refrigeration, the icebox was our only food cooler. Water from melting ice passed right down a tube that went through a hole drilled in the floor. And we were always successful in finding vendors of ice blocks when new refrigeration fuel was needed.

Mother poised to dump wastewater at one of our rural-schoolhouse campsites.

All in all, our 1949 homemade motorhome had most of the amenities of the 1990s version, just in rather primitive form. We made the most of this house on wheels and had some incredible experiences that created memories still vivid today. Without the motorhome, none of us kids had been farther than two hundred miles from Browns Valley, the distance to Minneapolis, and an occasional Christmas-shopping or relative-visiting adventure. With the motorhome, though, our range of affordable travel increased at least tenfold.

Our first trips were short ones within our home state of Minnesota. These were akin to shakedown cruises to identify any minor glitches in Dad's design and workmanship. I imagine some problems occurred, but nothing that we kids were aware of. We were simply reveling in a completely furnished house that moved down the road. Talk about kiddy heaven for the six of us, who ranged in age from about 3 to 13 years old! By the time we had toured the north shore of Lake Superior, and had walked across the mighty Mississippi River in only four strides, at its Lake Itasca origin, longer ventures were deemed safe.

During the next five years, we traveled to the Black Hills of South Dakota, to the Pacific Coast of Oregon, and to the inner reaches of the Ozarks of Arkansas, in addition to enjoying many nearby sorties. The scenery was always grand, especially to a group of kids who had never before been far from home, and for example had never seen a hill tall enough to be considered a mountain. A bit mysteriously, though, my most vivid memories are of the various misadventures that had little to do with scenery but much to do with Dad and his house-on-wheels creation.

Right to left: Author, father (Ward) and sisters Jean and Thalia. Orange Whale in background (1955).

Our trip to the Oregon Coast included a memorable misadventure. Cruising speed for the Orange Whale was a whopping 45 miles per hour on the flats, a bit faster on downgrades and noticeably slower on even the gentlest of inclines. The little six-cylinder engine could do no better, and the marginal reliability of mechanical brakes discouraged fast downhill travel. Thus, we spent almost twice as many hours to get from A to B as Anne and I need with our new Ford-powered Tioga.

The return trip included a tour of Yellowstone National Park. We kids giggled at the blurping sound and child-friendly messiness of boiling mud pots, stared deeply into the crystal-clear waters of hot pools, and marveled at the powerful regularity of Old Faithful Geyser. Mother purposely cooked very aromatic food for our meals, and not surprisingly bears responded by leaning against the sides of the Orange Whale in hopes of joining us for dinner. Bear claws left scratches in the faded paint. We wisely kept the front and back doors firmly closed.

We left Yellowstone to the northeast, by way of the ten-thousand-nine-hundred-forty-foot high Beartooth Pass, which proved to be almost too much for the GMC's six-cylinder power plant. We had to climb nearly four-thousand feet to get up and over the pass, and virtually all of this ascent was accomplished in the bus's two lowest gears. In fact, first gear (commonly called super low or granny back then) was needed most of the time. One could literally walk as fast as this gear moved the bus up the mountain. It took four hours to go sixty-four miles. But by this time the family was rich with the patience needed to endure slow travel, and thus stayed in the bus.

Dad's task, though, demanded more than just passive patience. He was repeatedly shifting between first and second gears, with the need to double clutch each time to avoid the grinding or even breaking of spinning gear teeth as they meshed into their new positions. A synchromesh or automatic transmission would have been a godsend, but these were not available back then. Fortunately, Dad was a very experienced and skilled truck driver, and we eventually topped the mountain pass, cruised down through Red

Lodge, Montana, and found a fine forested side road for the evening's camp spot.

The next morning we learned of the toll that yesterday's climb had taken on the bus's engine. That usually reliable engine would not start. By the time Dad had tried every technique and trick that he knew to get the engine running, the battery was dead. Next came a hike to the nearest home, where a friendly and cooperative rancher drove Dad back to the bus on a farm tractor, which was able to pull the bus fast enough to trigger ignition.

During the next several days that it took us to get home, the engine was shut off only at night. If a hill was available, we made it our campsite, inclined beds be darned, so we could coast the engine to a start the next morning. Otherwise, we found a campsite near a farm and thus became acquainted with several friendly country folks whose only request for remuneration for an engine-starting pull was a tour of the Orange Whale.

Such tours were very popular simply because our homemade motorhome was indeed a unique beast back then. We never once saw a similar rig on the road during all of our family trips, in contrast to the frequency of motorhome sightings on today's roadways. And more than once during our years of vacation travels, we were waved preferentially through restricted traffic zones, presumably because patrol officers thought the Orange Whale was a working school bus.

Once home where Dad's favorite local mechanic could evaluate the problem, it was discovered that the long slow tedious grind up and over Beartooth Pass had resulted in badly burned engine valves. A new set was installed, and the Orange Whale was ready to set sail anew.

Orange Whale at rest during a Minnesota winter.

As we kids aged to the point of developing other and often out-of-family interests and as the motorhome inevitably became less safe and reliable, Dad's invention was retired from its original use. During its autumn years, deer hunters bought the rig and used it as living quarters parked at various forest hunting grounds. Whatever sleek lines the tired old bus body could claim to retain were totally destroyed when the new owners cut a hole through the roof to accommodate the exhaust pipe of a stove installed for space heating. Even those silver fender straps and the helix twist to the body were lovely by comparison. I think we were all happy to have the bus disappear from town, rather than see this old friend age rather badly in the hands of less-than-loving care.

As a pre-teenage boy, I did not fully appreciate the cleverness and creativity that Dad displayed when he designed and built our family motorhome from that old school bus. In hindsight, though, I understand that he was indeed a man ahead of his time. Certainly, the motorhomes of today are more comfortable than that prototype of 1949 vintage, but I seriously doubt that families have any more fun in today's rigs than we had in our crippled-looking, slow-moving Orange Whale. Whatever the time frame, motorhome travel and sightseeing are delights to all those who appreciate experiencing landscapes at ground level rather than from stratospheric heights.

THE ORANGE WHALE GOES HILLBILLY

FAMILY TIES AND cohesion were very important to my parents — so important that no gene-sharing member should lie beyond the reach of a multi-day visit at least once in a lifetime. Telephone conversations and missives delivered by the U.S. Postal Service were nice trimmings, but literally pressing the flesh with handshakes and hugs and sharing vittles at a common table were the only true expressions of family unity. With the creation of the Orange Whale RV, our Browns Valley, Minnesota, clan was finally able to visit Dad's Aunt Mary, Uncle Louie, and their kids and extended family down south in the Ozark Hills of Arkansas.

All these decades later, I don't remember exactly where in the Ozarks we drove deeply into the woods to visit these kinfolks. But their place was sufficiently hidden that no evidence of a town and its offerings of civilization were within sight. Dad found a level spot to park the Orange Whale and that was our stationary home for several days. We two families mostly dined together, talked and talked about the many years of commonalities that earlier had been vicariously shared at great distances, and ventured forth for two memorable sorties from the woodsy setting when voices tired.

First we visited a nearby lake held in place by a small earthen dam. The time was summer — July I think. The weather was uncomfortably hot and drippingly humid. And the cooling water was so soothing that we Minnesotans stayed immersed in the sun-bathed lake too long. We spent the rest of our visit and some days beyond applying aloe-rich sunburn cream to nearly blistered bodies. Shared skin peeling became a game. Our Ozarkian kin were a bit surprised at the thin-skinned fragility of their visitors.

Next, we all emerged from the backwoods to enjoy a drive-in movie on what was advertised as "dollar night." The theater marquee advertised that any vehicle, no matter how many people therein, would be admitted for just one simoleon. My not-to-be-deterred Dad, who on an earlier trip in the Orange Whale had almost willed his house-on-wheels through the narrow tunnels of the Needles Highway in the Black Hills of South Dakota, wasted little time and palaver in convincing the theater manager that the Orange Whale and its dozen-plus passengers merited a one-dollar entrance. He was willing to pay a bit more, but with a negotiated compromise, Dad agreed to park in the back-most row in order to avoid screening the screen from anyone who might otherwise sit behind the Orange Whale. He parked parallel to the big silver screen, and we all scrambled from bumper to hood to roof to enjoy the movie (whose title I don't remember) while perched in a long row atop the Whale.

Now comes the memorable (for me!) and today laughable event which I suppose is the main reason I'm writing this story about our family visit to hillbilly country. For the seventy-plus years of my life to date, I have shared a rather personal, unforgettable Ozarkian happening with but one other Homo sapien … my wife. I've finally decided that others, even total strangers, might get a chuckle from what I'm about to write. Why take it to the grave! This story is about me and ticks.

The enlightened me of today knows that there are many varieties of ticks, some of which transmit diseases by attaching themselves to humans and leaving certain of their molecules behind while dining on our blood. I suppose there were multiple tick species when we visited the Ozarks too, but within our family then all ticks were simply wood ticks. And the Ozark forest was prime environment for a burgeoning population of wood ticks.

Sanitary plumbing at Aunt Mary and Uncle Louie's place consisted of a two-holer outhouse a short walk from the real house. During one visit while sitting on an opening of that two-seated throne, I discovered a blood-swollen tick firmly attached to and feasting on my scrotum. Yikes!! I'm sure I didn't think of the word *scrotum* back then, but decorum today asks for that word in this essay. Folk lore in tick country advised that the most effective way to remove such an unwanted visitor was to gently touch it with the hot end of a lit cigarette. Of course, I had none and wouldn't have risked burning such a tender pouch even if a cig had been at hand. So it was grasp, pinch, and pull, followed by stomp and squish on the outhouse floor. Then began the days of the embarrassment that I kept secret for so long.

The site of the tick bite was an unrelenting source of irritation — even worse than the after-effects of a visit from a Minnesota mosquito. For a couple of days (maybe longer?) I could last only seconds between scratching that itch. And if you think about body geometry, it's difficult to hide what's going on while in the presence of anyone else. I experimented with several techniques — for example, rubbing my legs together and repeatedly standing and sitting and turning away from others ... any motion that created some friction in the irritated zone! The most effective maneuver was a manual massage by a hand hidden in a front pocket of my blue jeans. No one seemed to sense my predicament, but still it was all so very embarrassing. I was probably not old enough to comprehend that I would want a healthy and functional scrotum later in life. Yet I was too unsure about what was transpiring to share my unease, even with Dad. I've come to think of that time as the two-day itch, not to be confused with the adult seven-year itch.

Much later in life, my entire body was threatened with extinction via a tick-bite disease called Ehrlichiosis. By comparison, the tick-caused scrotum scratch was a picnic. I never have returned to the wooded hills of the Ozarks, though.

*Dinner time in the Orange Whale.
Does that young boy look uncomfortable?!*

THE ORANGE WHALE PULLS A WEDGIE

A **WEDGIE, YOU** shout, in loud disbelief! How could an old school bus converted into an RV even know what today's American wedgie is!! Read on, my friends, to understand how this currently popular word and the Orange Whale came painfully tight together.

The Black Hills of South Dakota was the destination for one of the introductory Duffield-family trips in the Orange Whale. Mother's parents homesteaded there during the first decade of the 1900s, and Mom would have been born in their rustic isolated cabin if Grandma Weeks had not refused to give birth under such primitive conditions. She convinced Grandpa to move back to Minnesota for that event.

Our Orange Whale of the mid 1900s transported our family to the Grandparents' South Dakota homestead country. The drive from western Minnesota across the Great Plains of that state was a bit boring, being basically flat flat and flatter. Except for being drier and thus a bit less green, the landscape viewed from the Whale's windows looked a lot like home. We kids had the entire interior of the Whale for a playpen. But even that lost its appeal after hours and hours of 45 mph progress toward the real goal.

Ah, yes. There was one entertainingly memorable Great Plains event, triggered by the Orange Whale when we stopped in Pierre long enough to visit the State Capitol. Post tour of that remarkably lovely building, as Dad was about to shift into first gear, engage the clutch, and drive away, an elderly lady strode up to our rig and rapped on

Whale's side panel. In the knee-jerk reaction of a commercial school bus driver, which he was part-time at home, Dad reached right and pulled a handle that opened the entry door.

"Does this bus go to City Park?" our unexpected visitor asked.

"Don't know," Dad said through a chuckle-engulfed grin. "But if that park's on the way to the bridge over the Missouri, we'd be happy to give you a lift."

These nearly six decades later, I can't remember whether or not we drove that lady to her destination. But I do recall that that wasn't the only time and place when a local mistook the Orange Whale for a municipal city bus.

A couple hours after crossing the Missouri River, the Black Hills became visible as an indistinct broad dark-colored (ergo the name *Black* Hills) hump on the horizon. Later in life, I came to realize that this South Dakota version of lofty heights pales in comparison to most regions described as mountainous. But to us six kids who had never before experienced an elevation more than one-thousand feet above sea level, the seven-times-as-high summit of those distant dark hills would seem to float in suffocatingly thin atmosphere!

Mountains provided the literal and figurative highlight of our Black Hills trip. My most vivid memory, though, has little to do with landscape scenery and almost everything to do with Dad's curiosity and stubbornness as the captain of his house-on-wheels creation as we toured the Hills. The climactic event was a product of his can-do character.

The setting was the Needles Highway, a popular scenic route near Mount Rushmore, where erosion has shaped ancient (Precambrian for my geologist readers) granite into a forest of spires. We had already walked the gold-mine tour at Lead, seen the graves of Calamity Jane and Wild Bill Hickok in Deadwood, visited the Hill City Zoo, explored the underground wonders of Wind Cave, splashed in the geothermal waters of Evans Plunge, and watched a stirring rendition of Christendom's Passion Play at the outdoor Spearfish theater. Finally, it was time to experience the tunnels of the Needles Highway. None of us had ever before motored through a tunnel.

The adventure began at Sylvan Lake, where a large sign at the entrance to this winding roadway clearly warned that *trucks* and *trailer houses* were not allowed. Chauffeur Dad, however, badly wanted to master the tunnels and so he audibly rationalized that, "They must mean eighteen-wheeler rigs for trucks, Nita. Doesn't mention anything specifically about a school bus. So let's give it a go."

All tunnels were one-lane and narrow. Dad drove slowly into the first and successfully emerged at the far end. With confidence soaring, he steered into the next tunnel only to become wedged, about halfway through. The unforgiving granite walls were more closely spaced than the width of the bus. Orange Whale screeched to a stop, trapped between granite walls in contact with metal.

I fled to a bunk bed and buried my head under a sound-muting pillow. The metallic screeching reminded me of the eerie sound of fingernails raked across a blackboard at school. When I finally decided it was safe to emerge, my uncannily relaxed skillful (and lucky?) Dad was slowly backing our house on wheels without making the original Orange Whale wedgie even tighter. Once totally outside the granite walls, he managed to turn the Whale around by small forward and backward increments across the narrow mountain road. Mother directed traffic for an increasing number of sedans lining up behind us. Back at Sylvan Lake, we found the sides of the Whale newly decorated with horizontal scratches — long-lived reminders of the tunnel caper. The drive back to our hometown seemed quite relaxingly uneventful.

UPDATE: The original tunnels of the Needles Highway and its Highway 16 continuation of today are wider than those visited by the Orange Whale. Apparently even tourist buses can now avoid the thrill, stress, and embarrassment of a wedgie!

Mount Rushmore as seen through a tunnel of the Needles Highway area, 2013.

DAD DOES IT AGAIN!

THE FOLLOWING TRUE tale set in the mid 1940s exemplifies how this rather poor (financially) parent strove to provide his wife and children with some of life's luxuries — things beyond the bare necessities of food, shelter, and clothing. If you've read my earlier tales about the Orange Whale of an RV, which transported the family across geographies almost unimaginable to us kids, you've already been introduced to Dad's can-do solution to difficult mechanical problems. Now, I invite you to travel back in time to when I tired of my tricycle to the point of wanting a motorized version of play-time transportation. Similar to Dad's creation of a viable RV for our family vacations, his solution to placating his son's yearning for a motor bike was another feat of function over beauty.

    I was about six years old when I first saw, and immediately coveted, a Doodle Bug Scooter. My pestering eventually put Dad on a search that located a Doodle Bug junker. Not knowing the facts of then, my guess today is that he paid little or nothing for the relic he brought home. What had once been a bright red dream machine for a youngster to mount and master, was now the rusted hulk of pretty pathetic remains.

    These remains came with two inflated pneumatic tires — not much tread left, but serviceable. Where an internal-combustion engine had been mounted was now an empty platform beneath the operator's badly frayed seat cushion. A small lonely gasoline tank was strapped to the rear bar of the frame, apparently in search of a motor wanting energizing flammable fluid. Etched-in-metal evidence that rubber grips had once covered the steering handlebars was a distinct line between areas of moderate and heavy rust. The machine looked a lot like the one in this picture, which I've gleaned from the Internet.

This skeletal model appears to have the gas tank in front of the operator's seat.

But what I saw as a pretty discouraging disappointment, Dad viewed as a challenging project. For example, those were the days when most washing machines were powered by a gasoline engine of a size suitable for the available space on a Doodle Bug's frame. Dad found an abandoned washer, salvaged its engine, and bolted it into position.

The next substantial problem was how to transfer power from the engine to the rear wheel. A complete Doodle Bug did so via a V-belt that connected a pulley on the rear wheel to one on the engine's crank shaft. At engine idle, the belt hung loose. But at high-rev throttle, centrifugal force increased the effective radius of the crankshaft pulley, thus tightening the V-belt. How to create a similar transfer of engine power to the rear wheel of our lame machine was a challenge.

I (think I) remember seeing Dad retreat to the cab of his old Ford truck, and then hearing the click click click of its emergency-brake handle being pulled into locked position. My older readers may recall that an emergency brake for such a rig consisted of a vertical handle bolted to the floorboards. The operator pulled the handle, which ratchet-like clicked into a locked position to set the brake. A squeeze of the handle released the brake to its off position.

Within a few days, Dad salvaged such an emergency-brake handle from a trashed truck, and mounted it to the footboard of the

Doodle Bug in such a way that when ratcheted into a locked position it tightened a V-belt that connected engine pulley to rear wheel pulley. This completed all the components needed for my Doodle Bug to function. Was this machine a thing of beauty? NO! But it gave me the feeling of power and freedom that comes to a young kid when he revs that little rig to its top speed down a dusty gravel town street. I wish I had a photo of me in my pre-Harley mode, but I don't.

The key fact is that Dad's fix worked! Thanks for the memories, Dad.

ABOUT FACE AND FULL THROTTLE
A Pilot's Chilling Tale

WHENEVER THE WINTER season approaches, my mind wanders to youthful years of living with the snow and ice of the Upper Midwest. We all have cold-season stories to tell, and one of my favorites is about barnstorming in Dad's airplane. Recalling one particular escapade still induces a rush of adrenaline — and a bit of pride — nearly sixty years after the fact.

I grew up in the "Land of 10,000 Lakes," almost all of which freeze over thickly enough to support villages of fishing houses during long cold winters. The winter freeze also creates landing strips for small aircraft, wherever icy surfaces aren't covered with hummocky snow drifts.

During the mid 1950s, Dad and I flew a Cessna 120 out of a small private landing strip just east of our hometown of Browns Valley. An eighty-five-horsepower Lycoming engine was under the hood of this two-passenger tail-dragger aircraft. Wings were fabric-covered. The fuselage sported a shiny aluminum skin. There were no wing flaps to be used as a crutch when a pilot wants to fly at slower than what otherwise would be stall speed.

Our home-base landing strip was part of an alfalfa field owned by a farming friend. Zero services were available there, but the monthly rent for hangar space was zero, too, an acceptable tradeoff for a couple of barnstorming hayseeds. When winter snows came, we stopped flying (no skis). But when the snow was either light or late, we had exhilarating frozen-lake flying to enjoy.

Before another pilot might be tempted to fly toward the nearest body of frozen water to see if landing there is worth this print, that person should be sure there is no regulation against doing so on the chosen patch of ice. Once clear of this possible impediment, be sure to check the condition of the ice on foot. Dad and I did a preliminary walk and drive over the part of a lake where we intended to land. Once declared safe, we had the smoothest airfield imaginable. And if the lake was large, there was always a runway oriented directly into whatever wind might be blowing. No cross-wind landing challenges to deal with.

Teen-aged me and the Cessna 120 on a summer day.

In spite of these naturally built-in safeguards, there was one stomach-churning experience I will never forget. I was an eighteen-year-old college freshman at the time, home from Carleton for Christmas vacation. I had earned my solo pilot's permit at age fifteen and had logged about sixty hours since then. I was now about to take my first solo experience on a runway of ice.

The onset of western Minnesota's winter that year was snow-free, but characteristically cold. On the day of my near disaster, Mother and my sisters drove to our town's nearest lake, Traverse, for ice skating. Dad and I would fly out and join them.

Lake Traverse occupies part of a Pleistocene river channel eroded by glacial River Warren, which flowed southward from the melting, retreating North American ice sheet between about 14,000 to 11,000 years ago. Today, this long and narrow finger lake covers the bottom of the valley created by Warren. The midline of Traverse traces a twenty-mile gentle arc — part of the boundary between South Dakota and Minnesota. Width is a bit less than a mile.

At our alfalfa airport, we pushed the Cessna out of its hangar and completed a routine, but thorough pre-flight inspection. Following his shout of "clear," proper safety etiquette for the following, Dad hand spun the prop (there was no battery-powered cranking for this old plane) while I sat in the left seat at the controls. Magnetos engaged. Lycoming barked to life quickly and smoothly. Following a short taxi and then a catapult-style takeoff, aided, if not required by a noticeable hump about midway down the hayfield, we cruised a few hundred feet aloft toward the agreed-upon meeting spot, just a few miles distant.

Our runway of choice was oriented across the lake, at its south end, adjacent to where the family skaters were frolicking. Lack of wind invited a runway of any orientation. Dad made the first few touchdowns, while I followed his techniques by keeping light contact on the controls. I hadn't piloted at all for the past three months.

Then, I took control for a couple of touch-and-go circuits, with Dad poised to correct if my rustiness created any approach or touchdown problems. Rustiness quickly yielded to seemingly coordinated, well-oiled technique. I felt tremendous pleasure and release from the lingering trauma of the previous week's final exams.

When we rolled to a stop and shut down the engine for Dad to deplane, a father and pre-teen son skated over to chat. Three of us discussed the mandatory farm-country topics (weather, the past summer's crops, weather, pigs, weather, cows, weather, sheep, weather, and expectations for next year's crops) for awhile. Then the young boy interrupted with a question that apparently had puzzled him while watching our practice session.

He pointed and said, "Why don't those tires on your plane spin and slip when you speed up to take off?"

His father, Dad and I laughed, leaving him puzzled and maybe a bit annoyed. I assume his dad answered later. This kid wasn't familiar with the principal of the airscrew, that whirling propeller biting into the atmosphere to pull the plane forward, somewhat akin to a metal screw spinning its way into wood. But like all north-country folks, he was well aware of how car tires easily lose traction on ice.

Father and son skated off. Dad hand-cranked the 120 for me, and joined the rest of our family at the ice's edge where they now nibbled on snacks around a bonfire for warming hands and cheeks. I taxied to the east end of our cross-lake runway, turned, and with full throttle and spinning propeller once again experienced the feeling of freedom that comes with rising above the ground surface. I banked northward, up the long dimension of Traverse.

The safest direction to land would have been parallel to lake length. But I wanted to stay close to where the family skated, so my runway was where Dad and I had practiced. I made a low pass to recheck landscape where the shore rose gently along the left of my landing strip, while about two hundred feet to the right a parallel string of reed-covered islets poked a few feet above the ice sheet. I had a runway of smooth ice that was more than adequate for a competent pilot.

I gained elevation as I again flew in a broad arc to the north-northeast, and then turned south and finally west, lining up with the landing lane. My approach was faster than necessary. I suppose my lack of recent solo flying heightened my concern about stalling. But the icy runway was slipping quickly by as I descended. When the wheels touched down, it was clear that my approach speed had been faster than desirable, say nothing about necessary. Directly ahead, the west shoreline of the lake was nearing rapidly, and there were those pesky islets on the right, eliminating the possibility of a broad sliding turn toward a longer expanse of open ice. And it was too late for full throttle and a new takeoff.

I instinctively applied the brakes. But as the boy had pointed out, in his own way, the coefficient of friction between a rubber tire and ice is near zero. The west shoreline was coming into increasingly detailed focus, as though the windscreen was a camera's huge zoom lens. My mind flashed to the notion that the boy might get the last laugh, if indeed laughter would be appropriate once I came to rest.

Many thoughts must have raced through my mind during the next few seconds, and thanks to something, one of them was a bit of Dad's advice during the practice runs. With gritted teeth, I quickly pushed the right rudder pedal as far as it would move. The 120 went into a rapid sliding turnaround — a Cessna version of a demi-pirouette. I was now watching the east shore fade into the distance through the windscreen zoom lens, while the plane continued to slide, tail first, toward the west shore. I may have mumbled a thank you to Nature for creating such smooth ice for the small tail wheel now at the leading edge of my almost-out-of-control machine.

Then I applied full throttle and that efficient propeller airscrew quickly dragged me to a full stop. Motionlessness was such a relief that I simply sat quietly for a few minutes, engine idling. I realized that I needed more practice landings, now, while this learning experience was fresh in mind. But before taxiing back to the east end of the icy runway, I retreated to the visual shelter of the nearest island to complete my relief.

Dad, who was perhaps always overly trusting when it came to his son and machines, simply watched from the fireside. He probably was quite pleased that I had remembered his advice. My subsequent landings were near perfect.

Christmas was still a few days away, but I already had the only gift I really wanted ... the thrill of flying solo on ice for the first time. As fellow pilots know, any first solo experience is exhilarating.

So, inexperienced-pilot readers of this tale, remember to allow plenty of runway for the rollout on ice, or it better be about face and full throttle for you, too.

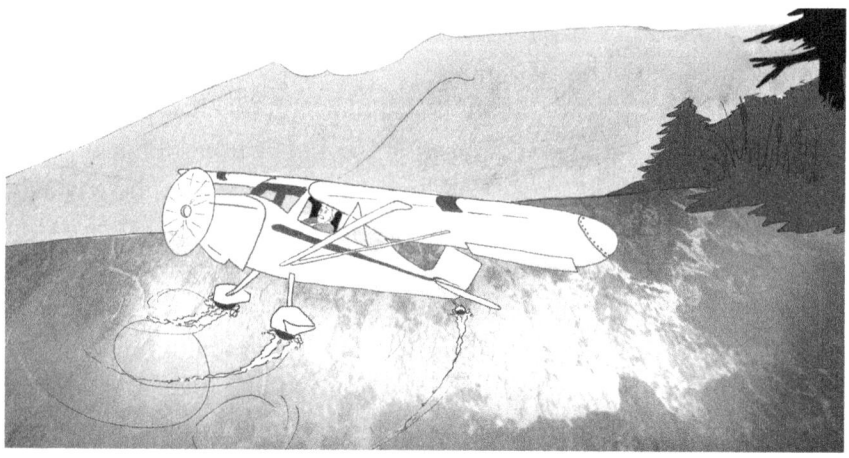

PICKING A CAREER WHILE PICKING ROCK

WITH TWO FARMING uncles like mine when I was a young teenager growing up in the hometown of Browns Valley, Minnesota, why would I need formal career counseling when that big decision time came to me as an undergraduate college student? Both of these avuncular men-of-the-earth mentors immediately took counseling credit when I announced my Carleton College decision to major in geology. Here's the back story.

Farming in west-central Minnesota always has been a pretty rocky way to make a living and raise a family. The soil there is rich, but its overall texture is a bit like lumpy pudding. Big hard rocks are mixed in with marly loam, and rocks are the bane of farm machinery. When a farmer's combine, hay-cutting sickle, or even sturdy four-bottom plow encounters a rock, that hard stuff of Earth usually wins, thereby sending the machine to a blacksmith for the equivalent of life-saving steel-welding surgery. The preferred solution to this scenario is to rid the farm fields of rocks, and this is where I enter the career-counseling tale.

The task called *picking rocks* is a tiring and tedious way to spend a day. In my youth, it commonly happened shortly before a crop was planted so the machine that "drills" seeds into the ground didn't suffer the fate that might befall the other aforementioned machines. As part of a typical rock-picking crew fielded by Uncle Willie or Uncle Clare, I was one of four whose job was to fan out to the sides of a slowly moving, tractor-pulled flatbed trailer and gather rocks cantaloupe size and larger. Some heavy rocks required two of us teens to heft it up onto the trailer. I was once even part of a crew where a couple of rocks required dynamite to be lifted out of the ground! But that's a blast of another story.

It takes little if any imagination to understand that being part of a rock picking-crew is boring. Once the topics of weather, cars, sports, food, girls and such were verbally dissected, there wasn't much more of interest to talk about. My mind then often drifted to what I was there to collect and carry. I made mental notes that most rocks were roughly round, as round as pieces of gravel washed down the small river that ran through town. Others were roughly flat, like the gravel stones that would skip two or three times across the surface of a pond when properly thrown. Colors varied from black to brown to red and dusty white. Some of the flat rocks carried an almost reflective silvery sheen. Some of the flat rocks were stacks of many flat layers somehow bound together. And some of the dark roundish rocks carried a whitish thin layer cutting right across the piece.

Whew! Somewhere in my mental meanderings about the whys and whats of this variety of rocks, I must have fantasized for a cold beer. Though not yet properly introduced to that beverage, I figured beer must be especially tasty because its consumption was strictly prohibited by my church. Sun-warmed water was the liquid that kept our rock-picking crew hydrated on any blistering humid Minnesota summer day.

Similar to the simple task of picking up rocks, wondering about them, the why and what of their variations in color, size, shape et cetera can also get boring. So yes, the best part of a typical rock-picking day was getting home to a hearty Mom-cooked meat-and-potatoes supper, followed by a cleansing therapeutic soak in the bathtub and enough sleep to be able to rise early for another day of … you know what.

Time to fast forward to my undergraduate college days: After briefly flirting with majors in math or physics, I settled on geology. Why? I can't honestly say what drove this decision several decades ago, but my best guess is that my childhood of picking rocks prompted a desire to finally understand the why and what of the broad spectrum of chunks I had laboriously toted to a creeping trailer. I also wanted to know why my hometown lay in a rather impressively broad and deep valley incised into extensive monotonous reaches of virtually flat plains. For the origin of every river in the state of 10,000 lakes, Minnesota myth gives credit to Paul Bunyan, who is purported to have created valleys by haphazardly dragging huge heavy pine logs to sawmills. One of the functions of college is to dispel myths.

Post-college, I now know that Canada is to be blamed (or credited?) for the rocks. Glaciers of geology's Pleistocene Ice Age bulldozed and carried this stuff hundreds of miles as they spread south from their Arctic origins. The sheets of ice repeatedly scraped across today's Canada and onto what would become the northern tier of USA states. When the glaciers melted back northward, their rocky loads were left behind. The good news, of course, is that the USA got an abundance of rich soil from Canada, too. If only the big pudding lumps could have been left way up north!

I also now know that a huge melt-water lake (Agassiz) accumulated in front of the most recent glacier as it retreated northward, and outflow from that lake eroded the valley where my hometown sits. Agassiz and its huge outlet river are now gone. But I digress.

When Uncles Willie and Clare learned that geology was the choice for my college major, they immediately announced career-counseling credit by claiming that rock-picking days had shaped my decision. The three of us joked about that a lot. I still smile to realize that their claim is valid to some degree — though to ever have admitted so to them would have spoiled the mental games we often played throughout our years together. They were great men and I miss them terribly!

PS: There's a truism often repeated in farm country where I grew up. It goes like this: *"The only crop a farmer can depend on to flourish every year is that of rocks in the field."* Repeated cycles of freeze/thaw freeze/thaw do in fact literally lift new unwanted machine-bashing rocks to the surface by spring of each year.

THOUGHTS ON A PhD THESIS PROPOSAL (OR) HOW I ALMOST GOT BOOTED FROM GRADUATE SCHOOL

AS A RIPE old septuagenarian, as the author of a fairly respectable record of published research results during a four-decade career in geology, and as a person currently basking in the comfortable position of a financially secure retirement from which only failing health or death can disrupt or dislodge me, I am now ready to share a graduate-school experience that might have short circuited the publications and retirement messages in the introductory phrases of this long sentence. Perhaps this essay will be of some use to present-day geology students aspiring to obtain MS and/or PhD degrees.

My graduate-school setting was the high-octane Department of Geology at Stanford University. Fueled with hope and enthusiasm, I arrived there in the fall of 1963 toting a Bachelor's degree, with a major in geology, issued earlier that year by Carleton College of Northfield, Minnesota. At Stanford, I was ready to begin scaling that one last rung on the academic ladder, which raises one to the lofty heights of a PhD. With that sheepskin in hand, I supposed I would be able to secure an intellectually challenging, physically exciting, and financially rewarding job in academia, industry, or government — perhaps with a focus of my own choosing. Back during the 1960s, jobs in geology were looking for people, rather than the other way around of more recent times!

I spent the first two years at Stanford in classrooms studying a variety of geology topics required for all of us new PhD candidates.

During year two of that period, each of us had to develop a proposal for an independent-research project, which would be the core of satisfying PhD requirements. Typically, four years in grad school would suffice for earning a PhD.

My proposal, like those of my graduate classmates, was supposed to demonstrate sufficient evidence that its author had the right stuff for designing, carrying out, and then publishing the results of a scientifically sound project in peer-reviewed geologic literature. Permission to continue on the path to a PhD depended on successfully explaining and defending the proposal before a panel of faculty critics. Members of my panel were an assigned advisor (a specialist in igneous petrology) plus three geology professors with other backgrounds.

Having come from the part of Minnesota where the surface geology is mostly drab sand, gravel, boulders, mud, and clay of Pleistocene glacial deposits, interrupted by some colorful coarse-grained Precambrian granite locally peeking through the young non-consolidated blanket, I had chosen to be what is called a "hard-rock" geologist, which has nothing to do with one's preferred genre of music. I simply wanted to study rocks hard enough to sing back when struck with a geology hammer.

During spring break of the second grad-school year, I ventured about twenty-five miles into northern Baja California, Mexico, and located a well-exposed pluton that had never yet been the subject of a focused geologic study. The outer contact of the body was obvious, even to a little-experienced field mapper like me. And the roughly hundred square miles of surface area were adequate for my fieldwork ambitions. So, this oval-outlined igneous plumb was mine to pick for a thesis area! I would be the first geologist to map the internal features of what I named the El Pinal Tonalite, after a local rancho. I planned to eventually explain this tonalite's role in the story behind the mountainous Mesozoic batholitic spine that crosses into Mexico from southern California. Or is the crossing from Baja California into Alta California? Rock formations do not recognize political boundaries.

When D-Day arrived, I felt well prepared with my proposal. The defense began smoothly, as I explained the where and what of my field area to the committee. Piece of cake, I mused to myself as the first hour or so of the big event flowed by without an upset.

Then an unanticipated series of questions from the structural-geology professor of the panel suddenly shattered my self-satisfied inner calm. Distilled down to a single notion, he wanted me to describe exactly what single critical question related to a large igneous intrusion I would answer through my research. He framed his query in several different ways as he tried to extract an acceptable answer from me. I thought I was responding adequately to each of his new angles, but ...

But I wasn't making any progress in our tete-a-tete. The other panel members watched and listened quietly. None of them was about to rescue me from my dilemma. Finally, in the confusion and frustration of an inexperienced young geology student — one could even say, a small-town country kid not long out of the woods — I blurted forth that I was going to carry out my proposed research project "So I can get that PhD and then land a good job."

A palpable silence immediately enveloped the room. One could have heard the proverbial pin drop, perhaps even onto a deeply carpeted floor. And then my thesis advisor asked me to leave. I fidgeted nervously in the hallway for several minutes, hearing raised voices through the solid oak door, until he joined me and said "Yes, you will be permitted to continue on the path to a Stanford PhD. But understand that more than one panel member was quite disappointed in your attitude about the value and significance of the PhD degree. Not all votes were thumbs up."

Whew!! So finally decades later, here I am to share a lesson learned back then — a lesson that I've carried with me ever since that stressful grad-school experience and what followed with my independent PhD study. There's a lingering quandary.

Should a PhD thesis proposal in geology be focused on answering a specific, and perhaps very narrow, question that is posed in advance of beginning any pertinent research? Or should a proposal be cast broadly enough that a researcher might discover information that could help answer multiple unanticipated questions and perhaps even illuminate entirely new questions that would emerge and beg to be explored further in mid-stream of research?

I accept a valid place for both paths in scientific research — a spectrum with end points that I call *DISCOVERY* and *VERIFICATION*. A research proposal based purely on discovery need have no specific advance plan, just a desire to study some situation to see what gives. Whereas research based solely on verification might simply work to further solidify a fairly well established hypothesis. Both avenues can advance our science.

My structural inquisitor of 1965 preferred the narrower approach to research, while I simply wanted to map, sample, and then deconstruct those samples to characterize the El Pinal pluton in as much detail as I was then capable of. I figured my hand-selected rock samples and their internal stories would lead me to answer questions about that pluton, and perhaps similar igneous intrusions, without any starting bias carried by an expected outcome.

Ironically, once the veil of mystery was peeled back by field and lab studies, I discovered that my thesis was fundamentally a study in structural geology. Neither I, nor my advisor, nor my structural geologist inquisitor would have predicted such an outcome in pre-fieldwork planning. By covering the ground on foot, collecting oriented samples to be studied with a universal-stage-outfitted microscope and thereby making many measurements of structural features both large and small, I discovered that the systematic orientations of platy plagioclase grains, elongate hornblende crystals, and flattened mafic inclusions together define a concentric pattern best explained as originating from the upward streaming of magma into a roughly six-mile-diameter zone around the core of the pluton — a zone that likely represents the roots of a ring dike. This ring dike might even have served as a passageway for magma feeding a volcanic eruption of caldera proportions. Any erupted magma to test that possibility would have been eroded away long ago. If you're interested, you can read about this story on pages 1351-1373 of the Geological Society of America Bulletin, v. 79, published in 1968.

If there's a common thread that ties together my post-thesis career in geology, it's that many El-Pinal-Tonalite-type surprises can be expected, in spite of well-thought-out project plans. Students take heed, and as the BSA motto advises, "Be prepared!"

REMEMBERING SIEMON "Si" MULLER

I SUSPECT THAT all students, whether they be academic types in a formal education setting or simply people navigating a less rigid learning path through life, encounter an unforgettable inspirational teacher or two along the way — an instructor in the broadest sense who becomes a permanent part of the student's existence.

One such hero of mine was a geology professor at Stanford University while I was a graduate student there in pursuit of a PhD degree, from 1963 to 1967. His name is Siemon William Muller, popularly called Si (pronounced like the word sigh). We were somewhat of an odd couple, since Si was primarily interested in learning what successions of layered sedimentary rocks could tell him about Earth's history, whereas I was on a track that led to a career studying igneous rocks, especially volcanic types. Nonetheless, we bonded as personal as well as professional friends.

Along my Stanford PhD path, I was required to complete a Master's degree thesis. Muller was assigned to be my Advisor. He directed me to map a brush-covered mountainous area of the California Coast ranges near the town of Coalinga. And his one guiding instruction that has stuck with me throughout my later career as a field geologist and is the motivation for now writing this essay was "Never ever locate a contact between different rock formations without actually walking along the path that will show up as a line on your geologic map." I could tell from his tone of voice and facial expression that he was serious about this advice. I did my best to follow it.

So instead of shortcutting some of my fieldwork traverses, I laboriously beat through the brush. There I encountered my first ever rattlesnake other than in scenes from an oater movie — scared the crap out of me — and learned after the fact that I was not allergic to poison oak. A friend who spent a day with me in the field wondered aloud if I knew what that plant was that I so cavalierly charged right through, pushing it aside with bare arms! With Muller's advice in mind, I endured all the scratches and scrapes and copious sweat that come with literally walking on a geologic contact in those Coast Ranges rather than following an easier path to the next convenient exposure. Muller was satisfied with my efforts and its product, and I was awarded my Master's degree from Stanford in 1965.

In addition to developing a friendship with this incredibly talented and personable man, his general advice about avoiding short cuts — the convenient and easier path — when dealing with important issues, often pops into my consciousness. Happy trails, Si, wherever you are! For more information about Muller, do a Google search for Siemon W. Muller.

A SPANISH LESSON IN TIME Helped Me Translate a Macho Rhyme

I hope readers of this essay won't be put off by the truly cutting nature of its punch line. As a kid who grew up with all the activities of a typical family farm of the 1940s, this particular style of lopping off (sometimes accomplished by knife and sometimes by rubber-band constriction) was part of the annual cycle of welcoming new animals into the herd. And as a human who is aware of the macho image that males of our species often project, I can appreciate the mindset that gave rise to my language lesson in Mexico.

WHEN I WAS a geology graduate student at Stanford University in the mid 1960s, the successful candidate for obtaining the PhD degree was required to demonstrate moderate proficiency in two foreign languages. Although the level of proficiency in the one-and-only foreign language I brought with me to Stanford was well above moderate, Latin was not accepted by the Geology Department. Lack of pertinent geologic literature in that tongue was the purported reason, although naturalists of the Roman Empire wrote many learned treatises about rocks and such centuries before Leland Stanford even thought to honor his son by establishing a top-notch university named for that lad. Sigh!

One of the early Roman scientists, who unfortunately witnessed the 79 A.D. eruption of Vesuvius at a lethal distance, would have the explosive style of that and many similar eruptions elsewhere named Plinian in his honor. But though I was on an educational track that would eventually lead me to study many Plinian volcanic deposits, my fluency in Latin was not accepted by Stanford standards. So, I enrolled in one-semester crash courses of German and Spanish. These were specifically designed to help graduate students like myself successfully clear the language hurdle. And they served that purpose for me and my classmates.

Within a few weeks of the course's termination, I forgot virtually all of the German that helped me jump the deutsche hurdle. But serendipitously my PhD thesis field area was in Baja California, Mexico. And in the lead up to my first south-of-the-border field season of mapping and collecting rock samples for lab studies, I practiced my rudimentary classroom Spanish through tapes and books, and by talking with Perfecto Mary, the Geology Department's rock-lab expert. Sēnor Mary was a native of Spanish-speaking South America. Our conversations were brief and quite repetitive. All these years later the one sentence I remember was his daily plaint, "Tengo mucho trabajo, pero poco dinero" followed by loud resounding laughter. Still, the inflections and cadence of his speech helped trained my ear for a relatively clear comprehension of what were strange sounds for someone who had never before been south of the border. My only previous exposure to Spanish came from watching TV shows of the Cisco Kid.

So armed with the sad story of trabajo and dinero, plus several other handy phrases mostly about the weather and such trivia, I drove south into the back country of Baja alone. I set up camp, a tent that served as home and office, forty miles south of the Mexican border town of Tecate (beer drinkers should recognize this name) at the middle of an extensive body of igneous rock, which I was to study. My only human neighbors within a several mile radius were Sēnor and Sēnora Amador and their fourteen children. The oldest child, Domingo, was forty. His name would be assigned to the first cat that my wife and I would soon adopt back in Stanford student housing. The youngest Amador was four. Obviously the father of this brood was quite an active amador, with living evidence of considerable fertility and staying power.

The family welcomed me onto their cattle-ranch land. I often encountered a couple of the older vaquero male children (who were much older than me) during my daily on-foot traverses across the landscape as I mapped and collected rock samples. Our conversations were necessarily brief and mundane. They knew no English and my Spanish was still rudimentary. So talk was limited to hello, how are you, nice weather and such. Then they would trot away on their caballos as I hefted my rock-filled backpack. The Amador family and I parted ways at the end of that first field season with embraces and my clumsy attempts to say that I would return the following summer.

Back at Stanford I continued studying Spanish through tapes, books, and conversations with Perfecto Mary. My vocabulary expanded beyond weather and how-do-you-do. I began field season two with hopes of having extended conversations with my Mexican friends.

Be patient. I'm getting to the punch line of this tale. It came on a day when I met Domingo and Eugenio, the next-to-oldest son, during one of my rock-collecting cross-country hikes. Remember that they knew me as a young adult living alone for weeks and weeks and weeks. As they broached that day's topic, I sensed their puzzlement of the fact that I hadn't yet visited two, perhaps similarly lonesome, young señoritas who lived at a neighboring ranch. After a couple of repetitions, I came to realize that they were asking why I didn't seek out some female comfort, or whatever their words were to express this idea. I knew what they meant. They were two of fourteen products of the topic being explored.

Wanting to impress my friends with my use of their language, I silently recalled that the Spanish verb *estar* (to be, in English) generally carries a connotation of some uncertainty. By contrast *ser* (also, to be, in English) carries a connotation of certainty. So I proudly announced in the first-person singular of *ser*, "¡Soy casado!" hoping to have said that I was married and indeed I intended to loyally and truly stay that way. My pronouncement triggered high-decibel laughter.

In loud unison came their rapid boisterous rejoinder of "¡Pero no capado!" again followed by raucous laughter.

And I got it. My vocabulary included their verb whose English translation was a significant part of my childhood upbringing on farms. So we all had a good laugh.

When I arrived back at Stanford where my wife Anne held forth, I related the entire tale. And of course I emphasized the reason for my use of the Spanish verb *ser*!

TRANSITION TIME, SMOOTHED BY LIMERICK RHYME

During many years of my post-PhD career with the United States Geological Survey in Flagstaff, Arizona, I was one of several USGS volunteers who ran an annual earth science training course for science teachers of the local public school system. Training consisted of several evening lectures in Flagstaff, followed by multi-day camp-out field trips for hands-on experience with geologic materials (i.e., rocks and such). As I became better and better acquainted with teachers in the field and around the evening campfires, my mind (inexplicably?) focused on a limerick-writing track. Here are a few samples. The teachers named will recognize themselves and their behavior foibles!

A masculine teacher called Ken
For females did have a strong yen
When his sweetheart fantastic
Turned out to be plastic
He no longer ranked her a ten

A cute science teacher named Julie
On field trips can get quite unruly
While singing one night
Round the campfire light
She gave hugs all around, oh yes, truly

A chemistry teacher called Flaccus
To get our attention would whack us
If this didn't work
An alternative quirk
Was exploding balloons to attract us

~~UTTERLY WARM MEMORIES~~
Too Sappy
~~UTTERLY WARM MAMMERIES~~
Maybe
~~UDDERLY WARM MEMORIES~~
Closer
UDDERLY WARM MAMMERIES
Yes!

THOUGH ONLY LATE October, I watched the first Flagstaff snowfall of 2012/13 wintery weather coat my lawn a few days ago. It melted away within hours, but even briefly once again seeing that white stuff triggered memories of having grown up in cold winter country with serious amounts of snow that stayed for months once it began to accumulate. That's what happened during my childhood years in Minnesota. Now I was in Arizona.

Close your eyes, and create the mental year-round picture of a characteristic Arizona landscape — one typically imagined by most out-of-staters. You will likely visualize some combination of ocotillo, heat, haboobs, heat, prickly pear, heat, gila monsters, heat, saguaro, heat, rattlesnakes, heat, cholla, heat, scorpions, extreme heat. It's a bit less hot during the winter months, but …

Such a blazing not-so-people-friendly image fits much of the state. Yet during the winter months, a forested mountain town in the north part of Arizona sits at an elevation that can cause precipitation to fall as the solid phase rather than in liquid droplets. That was my town. And yes Virginia, there is a wintery Santa Claus season in that part of

Arizona — an environment where Santa brings weather foreign to our lowlanders, who are more accustomed to worrying about the health of an air conditioner than the BTU rating of a furnace.

With snow, the tree-covered slopes of a giant extinct volcano called San Francisco Mountain — which looms nearly 6,000 feet above the north edge of 7,000-foot-high Flagstaff — are open for exhilarating steeply downhill winter sports. Gentler bumps in the adjacent landscape are runways for sleds, toboggans, and other slippery-bottomed contraptions that can be mounted by humans. Through the street-side window of my house, I can see neighbors strutting briskly by with poles and cross country skis carried over their shoulders — headed for some kick-glide exercise in the National Forest surrounding the town. Chamber-of-Commerce types temporarily convert a hilly city street into a snow-play zone. And as lemming-like creatures on a determined march, thousands of desert-elevation Arizonans create hours-long traffic jams creeping uphill toward Flagstaff for an opportunity to play in snow.

Once there, the routine for daily recreation begins shortly after a large orange orb called the sun peeks above the eastern horizon. Hours later, happily exhausted snow bunnies end their day in a dazzling array of orange and red tail-lights of vehicles headed to a motel or the guest bedroom of a Flagstaff friend. Some version of this wintertime madness has happened each of the thirty years that I've lived in Flagstaff. And I expect it to continue until the day my ashes are spread across a horse pasture, wherever that may happen.

Still a latent product of my Minnesota origins, I watch the annual Flagstaff winter frenzy with amusement and in near disbelief. The mania brought on by a bit of snow at barely freezing temperatures is laughable compared to the cold and snowy bite of winter where I grew up. Consider this. A small Minnesota village named Embarrass is known for often experiencing the coldest winter temperatures of the entire lower forty-eight states. Google that up if you doubt me. My home town of Browns Valley isn't much warmer. Most native Upper Midwesterners would be a bit embarrassed to call a Flagstaff winter … well … winter.

When I was a kid, we cold-hardened folks experienced extended periods when daytime temperatures never rose above zero Fahrenheit and when nighttime lows sank into the abyss of minus forty, the unique number where the Fahrenheit and Centigrade scales coincide. Snow accompanying such cold — there was commonly more than plows could keep up with — was more often an enemy to be conquered in order to go about the daily business of living, rather than an ally in recreation. Well sure, Minnesota folks also play in their snow — but only after daily life-sustaining chores are done.

I grew up in family-farm country. And still today, sixty years later, one of my most vivid memories of those times remains the seemingly simple task of keeping one's fingers from being frostbitten while doing the chores. Twice every winter day, chickens had to be watered and fed, and their eggs gathered. A slurry of ground oats had to be stirred up and sloppily offered to hungry hogs. Bales of hay had to be opened and spread across a snow-covered pasture where sheep and beef cattle roamed. And dairy cows had to be brought into the barn for milking.

Gloved or mittened hands invariably tingled close to numbness from the cold of dealing with the care and feeding of chickens, hogs, sheep, and beef cattle. In stark contrast, the task of milking dairy cows was a welcome warming-up event. Now you can begin to understand why the word *udderly* appears in the title of this essay.

I had to milk six Holstein cows. These gentle and remarkably intelligent critters had built-in clocks that told them to come to the barn when the big orange sun rose in the east and again when it began to set in the west. When I swung the barn door open, they single-filed in, each to her unique station as though a name-tag positioning arrangement was somehow involved. I have never understood this bit of orderly family-farm milk cow etiquette. But it's real.

I clicked stanchions closed over necks to keep the cows stationary during milking. I shackled the hind legs of known kickers — those who didn't much like having their teats pulled. My farm-boy days were during a "primitive" era, when affordable mechanized milking machines for a small family operation gathered dust as half-baked ideas on an inventor's sketch pad. So at cow after cow, I sat on a low one-legged stool, held a clean stainless steel bucket sandwiched tightly between my knees, grasped two of the four teats hanging from the milk-engorged udder, squeezed gently from top to bottom, and watched milk audibly splashing into the pail. Frigid fingers from the outdoor chores were quickly warmed by contact with a Holstein milk reservoir and its fleshy taps. Human-made gloves and mittens are second-rate heaters by comparison.

Hand milking a cow made great exercise and conditioned my grip better than a stress ball ever could. First, my hands enveloped the two near-side teats. Then I squeezed one and released. Squeezed the other and released. Repeat. Then I grasped the two far-side teats. Squeezed and released. Squeezed and released. Repeat. Back and forth. Back and forth. The rhythm and sound of milk splashing into the pail was musical. And oh, my hands were so warm!

As I moved down the lineup of cows, rodent-control barn cats watched closely, knowing I would soon offer them a fresh warm treat. As a teaser for them and a fun diversion for me, I occasionally aimed an airborne squirt of milk across the room toward gaping cat mouths that were incredibly adept at catching the white spray. At about fifteen minutes per cow, this regime continued for nearly ninety minutes before all udders were drained, and I released the cows back outside to munch on some of the hay spread across the snowy pasture.

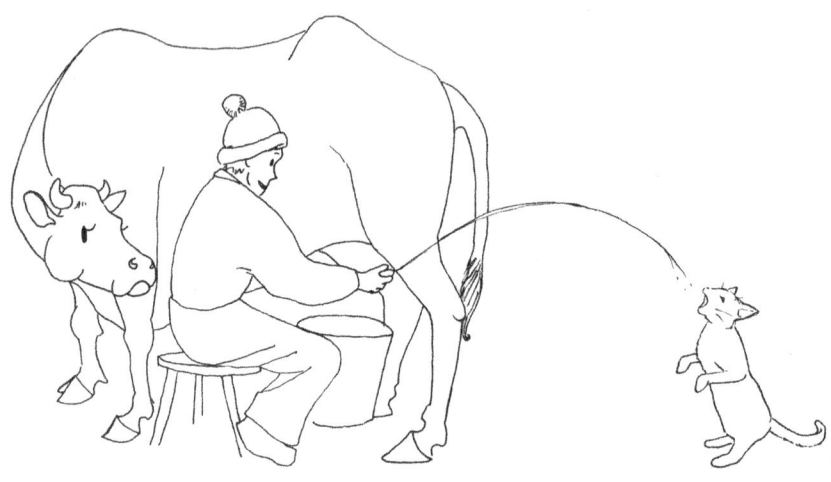

I wouldn't say that I want to return to this type of youthful farm-boy life, now that I'm a septuagenarian. But the memories are mostly pleasant. And they remind me how benign a Flagstaff winter is by comparison. My Michigan-raised wife has a similar take on Flagstaff weather.

She and I keep a pretty chilly winter-time bedroom in our Flagstaff house. It's a contribution to help reduce the human carbon footprint for the benefit of planet Earth. Plus, we enjoy slipping into a cold bed to rediscover how quickly heat radiated from a human body can warm the space between blankets. More often than not, my hands stray in search of udder heat during the warming-up period. I guess they tend to linger, too. And no matter how many times I explain this behavior as the involuntary action of a youthful farm-boy's winter-time experience — as involuntary as a heartbeat or another breath, and as involuntary as cows coming in to be milked with the rising and setting of the big orange sun — my tolerant wife and bed partner of nearly fifty years remains amusedly skeptical.

Whatever! Enjoy your winters, my readers, whether they be frigid or barely freezing. And practice the advice of Prairie-Home philosopher Garrison Keillor. "Be well. Do good work. And keep in touch." But use good judgment in selecting whom and what you touch!

NUMBER TWO MUSINGS

AS I EXERCISE my computer keyboard for this essay, it's Halloween time again. It's a festive season of ghosts, goblins, zombies, haunted houses, and witches riding brooms. A time when scary visages are carved into an untold number of bright orange pumpkins, whose nighttime candle-lit innards decorate home window sills and entry stoops. A time for young costumed children to knock on neighborhood doors and hold forth with open bags, into which sugary edibles are dropped for later (generally unneeded) consumption. A time for teenagers to feel free to pull such pranks as soaping windows and (where I grew up more than sixty years ago) toppling an outhouse while gleefully imagining that some poor soul is inside tending to business as what was comfortably horizontal suddenly becomes messily vertical.

Oh. What a headache!!

Halloween is also a time, for those kids who can afford the necessary ammunition, to decorate treed landscapes by throwing rolls of toilet tissue that unfurl during flight, resulting in white ribbons festooning whole city lots. We call this Halloween trick TPing, and my recollections of this silly prank prompt me to explore the topic of how TP tissues are more generally used.

An example of pretty successful TPing!

An essay about human waste and the business of using TP for the follow-on cleanup may be tough to market, but I'm writing it anyway. Any loss of a lavish advance and royalties be damned! The idea of stirring my knowledge of things poo into the published public cesspool of literature has scented the recesses of my thoughts for way too many years to delay my yearning for action any longer. Besides, at seventy-plus-years-old and counting, I may soon descend into a pit of a hopelessly scrambled English language. The time for action is now, while I can still produce a grammatically correct sequence of subject-verb-object, adorned with properly interspersed phrases and modifiers, all of which is terminated with a period, question mark, or exclamation point.

As a PhD scientist (the certificated proof of which is called poo paper by jealous detractors), part of the structure for any successful essay calls for definition of key terms up front. Now, poo may not strike you as something remotely associated with the phrase "up front," but let me clarify terminology before delving into some of the scatological history and sociological aspects attached to this word.

My copy of Webster's Collegiate Dictionary doesn't list poo. But aren't Google searches wonderfully informative! With apologies to sensitive readers (and to the popular homophonous Winnie), the Urban Dictionary's definition is *the noun used to describe the amount of sh*t that is passed in any single bowel movement. An additional o (or two or more) describes an increased volume per event.* Just imagine the elephantine size of a pile of pooooooo! In my lexicon, poo is also a verb. It is also known as number two.

Was it unique to rural grade-schools in Minnesota, where I grew up? Or did you non-Minnesotans also have to ask to visit the loo by raising your hand with an index finger and its long neighbor extended for permission to go poo? A lone index finger requested tinkle time. Teacher would nod okay. Lake Wobegon etiquette demanded that no words be spoken.

New students learned this digital signing system from their veteran schoolmates. Where the first-ever students learned the code seems to be the stuff of murky lore. My teachers never volunteered an explanation of who invented (and why) number two for poo. Neither did my parents. But my gentle, wise, and understanding maternal grandmother did.

As a child, I spent tons of time at Grandma and Grandpa's farm. Watching the uninhibited barnyard antics of their chickens, cows, dogs, ducks, cats, horses, pigs, and sheep inevitably created a lot of questions about animal behavior in the mind of a young naïve boy. Grandma always encouraged me to ask about whatever was on my mind. So she wasn't a bit surprised when I asked why pairs of these critters liked to ride each other, or when I popped the question of why poo was known as number two at school.

I blurted forth my poo enquiry while Grandma and I were sitting on the entry steps of their small clapboard home. She stopped washing chicken poo from the day's freshly gathered eggs, dried her hands on her ankle-length tent-cut dress, sat me on her knee, and began. "So, Wendy," she said in a soothing voice where condescension never roamed. "Today you want to know why poo at your school is number two." She tousled my hair as she spoke. "For a seven-year-old, you're growing up pretty fast. Seems you want to know all the whys behind the ways of people and other animals." During some of my earlier visits we'd already covered the basics of farm-animal breeding and birthing, with hints of how humans fit into that overall rodeo of bareback rides.

I nodded and grinned, exposing the gap of a missing incisor whose recent loss had been rewarded with coins left by a night-time visit of the tooth fairy. This time, though, I had learned the un-fairyed version of how money came to be placed under my pillow as I slept. Dad had mistakenly included his favorite steam-locomotive flattened penny in the loot. Santa Claus was still real to me, but now I hoped to learn the adult truth behind yet another of the many growing-up mysteries.

"Yes Grandma," I said snuggling deeper into her lap. "Why is poo number two?"

She didn't have to urge me to pay attention, like my school teacher often did. Grandma's stories were always fascinating. As I looked up into her face, she summoned her special wizened twinkle of sky-blue eyes and pointed to the old two-holer, a tired-looking building that sat well away from the house in the prevailing downwind direction. My eyes followed her finger toward an eye-catching sight in an otherwise ordinary farm scene. In an attempted spruce-up, Grandpa had painted that shabby outbuilding bright orange to match his Allis Chalmers tractor. Where I grew up, many farmers were like that with regard to their brand of tractor. John Deere green, Farmall red, Minneapolis Moline yellow, Allis Chalmers orange. It was pretty easy to guess the favored tractor brand by the color motif of a farmer's buildings.

Grandma continued. "When you go to that outhouse. When you drop your bib overalls to the floor, then your undies, and sit over an opening to take care of business, what's the first thing out?"

Grandma and Grandpa didn't have indoor plumbing for a flush toilet. They also didn't have electricity or a pressurized water system. The eerie orange flames of kerosene lamps lit the house at night, and human effort at the handle of a well's pump lifted ground water to the surface for human and farm-animal consumption alike. On many days, a harnessed Great Plains wind helped lift water, too.

I closed my eyes and puzzled silently, trying to re-create the sequence of events in Stormy, the name Grandpa had painted in white across the door of the single-purpose shed. I'd never before thought about the order of body-waste expulsion on the many occasions of occupying Stormy's throne. What kind of mind would be doing that? Besides, my keen sense of smell always said *do your business fast and flee this stinky place*. I gritted my teeth to help with concentration.

Let's see. Sit, relax, and … Aha! "I've got it Grandma," I yelled, eyes open wide. "Number one always starts first. Always. So number two has to be poo!!"

"That's right," Grandma said, as she lifted me to my feet and went back to washing eggs so they wouldn't be rejected by the commercial buyer in town. "You're a smart boy Wendy. I bet you'll be a teacher some day. Now, run down to the barn and tell Grandpa it's time for lunch."

I can't wait to tell my classmates, I thought, flashing my gap-toothed open-mouth smile at Grandma, before sprinting toward the big building topped with a rooster-shaped weathervane.

Early Homo sapiens were presumably about as self-conscious and socially concerned as my pet dog when Nature called for number-two action. Squat, squeeze off the last tapered sausage-like link, and walk away relieved. Having witnessed my dog's occasional misstep, one should never *back* away from a fresh poo pile.

As time passed, increasingly fastidious *Homo sapiens* introduced the technique of a post-poo wipe. The advantages of this practice had become obvious to many of the human senses and sensibilities. Though rarely (if ever?) appearing in public print, treatises of wipeology make for educational reading, and as you will soon discover, may even correlate with the strength of an economy.

Now ... please look beyond the broad range of toilet paper shapes, thicknesses, absorbency coefficients, and so forth that exist in different present-day cultures. Instead, consider the characteristics of the two primary folding practices applied to a typical roll of perforated American stock. There are two fundamentally different techniques. Adherents of camp A neatly fold a few sheets along the lines of perforation to create a multi-ply tool for the job. Folks of camp B, however, are risk-taking wadders. They tear off a random length of the paper and scrunch it into a mass that fits the shape of the hand. The personality contrasts between adherents of A and B carry fundamental Freudian behavioral connotations whose discovery I leave to the reader.

The true sophisticates of *folders* are keenly aware of a substantial strength-anisotropy factor that can determine the number of sheets needed for a clean-hand wipe. Some brands of paper are much stronger across, than along sheets ... a bit like the popular string cheese that tears so easily in one direction. So, if a *folder* wants to minimize the possibility of dirty digits because he or she held a multi-ply tool in the weak orientation, appropriate pre-wipe problem-solving and follow-on action are essential. Thus, with some thought aforehand, the digits of a *folder* can stay clean and even reduce the poo-time carbon footprint by using fewer (properly oriented) sheets per successful operation. *Wadders* cancel out the anisotropy factor because their individual sheets are arranged in random orientations during the wadding process.

A third technique of paper usage exists, although to date only a few practitioners of this style are publicly known. A *roller* wraps the paper around and around and around the hand until it is swaddled as completely and tightly as an Egyptian mummy. This is clearly wasteful of paper, but a clean-hand wipe is guaranteed for even the most spastic of pooers.

Yet another variation of paper usage speaks directly to prevalent supply-and-demand conditions within a society.

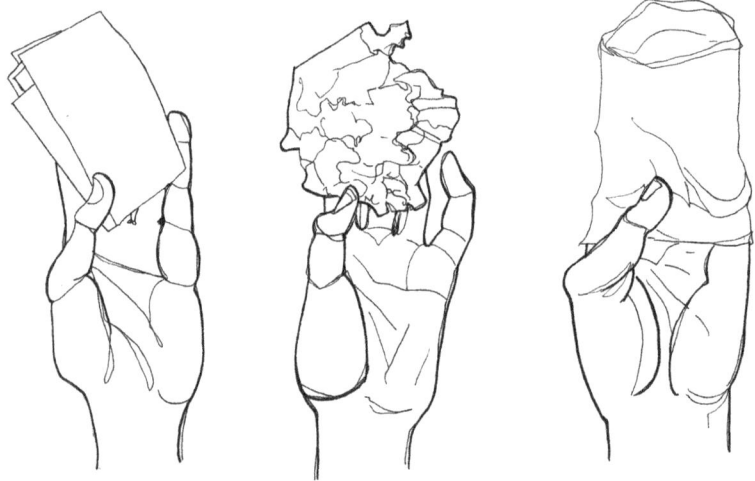

No job is finished until the paper work's done. Hmmmm. Which technique should I use?

Your attention please! For three adult years, I lived in Hawaii, where many of life's necessities arrive by ship. Island longshoremen know that being able to control the flow of these goods is a powerful bargaining tool. Ergo, strikes are frequent. During one protracted work stoppage, I learned that the human capacity for hording and thieving is not far below the surface veneer of an otherwise civilized society. Once such staples as salt, pepper, rice, soy sauce ... and yes even toilet paper ... were in increasingly short supply, they began to disappear from restaurants and other non-traditional shopping centers. The dirty truth was that some islanders dined out for the sole purpose of pilfering. Silverware was not at all coveted the way butt wipe was!

Back then, my friend Jeff, who had lived in Hawaii his entire life, laughed when I expressed surprise about this aberrant human behavior. "Happens with every long strike," he said. "At first, when supplies are getting kind of tight, folks don't spice their food as much. Maybe they eat less rice per serving. The popularity of our locally produced tasteless pasty poi sometimes makes a comeback. Fruit on wild trees doesn't go to waste. That kind of thing. People make do. As we locals say, "It's no big thing."

"Common sense," I said.

"But here *is* a big thing that you may not believe because you haven't lived here long enough to be pushed to this extreme. Folks eventually make their toilet paper do double duty."

"What do you mean by double?"

"Use a little imagination," Jeff said. "Another of our local sayings is that y*ou know the Island economy is in the toilet when you have to use both sides of the paper.*"

I've briefly experimented with the two-sided folder technique, with varying degrees of success. One-handed manual dexterity is a huge plus.

In addition to Halloween, voting for a host of national, state, and local offices is just days away as I compose this essay. Social, economic, and national-defense positions voiced by some of the candidates at all levels, are as frightening as the most ghoulish costumes and behavior of Halloween ilk. The less-than-kind side of my political self smiles at the thought of somehow forcing certain elected or wanna-be officeholders to use the two-sided technique for the rest of their lives. Poo power to the people!!!

GREEN ELECTRICITY FROM SEWAGE

HAVE YOU EVER thought that when you flush the toilet, once you've finished with your business, you could be helping to generate electricity? If you're a normal and reasonably fastidious person, the probable answer is a resounding no.

Well, what that simple flush can accomplish today holds energetic possibilities unthought of, if not unthinkable, just a few years ago. The technique of flashing liquid sewage to high-pressure turbine-driving steam exists right here in the USA. The story behind reality is contained in the history of exploiting geothermal energy at a place called The Geysers, about fifty miles north of San Francisco, California. It's also a tale of two seemingly unrelated nagging problems that unexpectedly find a common solution that is simultaneously good for business and the environment. If this sounds too good to be true, read on.

Geothermal energy is simply the earth's natural heat, vast amounts of which continuously make their way to the surface and dissipate into space. There's still plenty of this internal heat for humans to harness, in spite of the fact that cooling has been underway since the creation of our planet, about 4.6 billion years ago.

Geothermal energy is commercially exploitable from the relatively low temperatures found only a few yards beneath your yard, all the way up to several hundreds of degrees Fahrenheit, often found at readily drillable depths within the roots of volcanic and earthquake-prone regions. It's right there waiting to be tapped.

In 1904 at a place called Larderello in Tuscany, Prince Piero Ginori Conti was the first person to generate electricity by harnessing geothermal steam. The rest of the world was a bit slow to follow this creative Italian's lead, but by the late 1950s and early 1960s, geothermally powered electrical plants were in operation at several places around the globe. One of these places was The Geysers, an area with hot springs and fumaroles in the California Coast ranges. This site of geothermal manifestations, which was originally developed as a spa for adventuresome vacationers, was eventually transformed into a major producer of electricity.

As any entrepreneur would agree, free fuel for driving a turbine generator is good for the company's bottom line. And geothermal steam is virtually free, once production wells and a network of steam-transporting pipes are in place. With dirt-cheap fuel and other incentives as driving forces, during the 1980s The Geysers grew to be the largest geothermal electrical development in the world. At its peak in the late 1980s, about two thousand megawatts of generating capacity had been installed and was running. This large development was capable of generating enough electrical juice to satisfy the sometimes voracious thirst of a "typical" USA city with two million people.

For comparison, two thousand megawatts is roughly the electrical-generation equivalent of two Glen Canyon dams at full bore. At The Geysers, electrical power comes without drowning a preciously beautiful canyon in the process. Deer and cattle grazed the hilly pastures at The Geysers before geothermal development, and they still do so today.

The future of the geothermal-energy industry at The Geysers looked rosy in those halcyon 1980s. Steam was streaming. Turbines were spinning. And profits were accruing. Then, the inevitable(?) consequence of over-zealous exploitation, lack of foresight and planning, and perhaps other unrecognized factors turned rose petals brown.

The rate at which steam was being removed was noticeably depleting this source of free fuel. There were several companies producing steam, and together they simply had too many straws in the milkshake. Roughly four hundred production wells, ranging from about five thousand to nine thousand feet deep, were removing steam at a rate much faster than Nature could replace it. The subsurface geothermal resource, a network of interconnected steam-filled cracks and fractures within a large volume of very hot rock, was literally going dry. Steam pressure in wells began dropping. By 1992, steam production could drive only about one thousand megawatts of the two thousand installed capacity.

What to do? It was apparent that sources of "make up" water were needed — water that could be pumped underground to keep the fractured hot rock saturated with high-pressure steam. However, locally available sources of stream and shallow ground water, augmented by some steam condensate at the bottom end of the electricity-generation cycle, were woefully inadequate for the geothermal needs. Steam production continued to drop. The future seemed pretty bleak.

Meanwhile, just over the crest of the first Coast Range ridge to the northeast, communities along and near Clear Lake were in need of new ways to properly dispose of their treated sewage. The water quality of this large lake, a popular tourist destination as well as home to a growing permanent population, was being compromised by the inevitable invasion of sewage, albeit treated, percolating from wetlands and other holding ponds. Something had to be done before the metaphorical goose that laid the golden egg, in the form of a stunningly beautiful freshwater lake, drowned in the waste generated by people drawn to the area.

At this point, the interplay between supply and demand led to a deal advantageous to all stakeholders — and pretty friendly to Mother Earth, too.

Geothermal developers recognized that treated sewage could be used to artificially replenish the subsurface supply of steam at The Geysers. In terms of thermal energy, there was, and still is today, an immense resource in the ground. The only real problem was that dwindling supply of steam, the stuff needed to carry calories to the surface where they can be put to work.

Negotiations led to a partnership among county sanitation districts, the Northern California Power Agency, and private companies heavily invested at The Geysers. In the end, construction of a pipeline got underway in 1995. The initial pipe began to carry the wastewater of treated sewage to the southern part of The Geysers by late 1997. At the delivery end, wastewater is injected underground through wells, which are distributed to try to optimize the subsurface flow to production wells. The relatively cool injected fluid becomes heated through contact with hot rock, and it reappears as high-pressure steam at nearby production wells.

It's too early in the process to know what the long-term outcome will eventually be. But results to date are encouraging. The fall from two thousand megawatts of output to about one thousand by 1992 has since been stabilized at about eight hundred.

Who knows? Once the results of more years of injection are available, perhaps wastewater could be injected at even higher rates. We humans seem to have a knack for producing prodigious quantities of liquid sewage. And there's certainly still plenty of thermal energy in the rocks, waiting to be lifted to the surface as turbine-driving steam.

So, next time you rise up from your throne and flush your efforts down the drain, feel uplifted and heartened by the fact that someone doing the same thing in northern California is helping to keep the USA's electrical grid charged with dancing electrons.

You might also feel a warm glow knowing that electricity generated by geothermal steam, be it natural or the product of injected wastewater, releases virtually no greenhouse gases to the atmosphere, in stark contrast to those dirty coal- and hydrocarbon-fueled plants.

Flush to flash. Effluent to affluent. One person's waste can be another person's treasure.

TWICE BITTEN BY MARCH MADNESS

MARCH 8, 2009: "Hey couch potato," Anne said in a voice tinged with impatience. "How about we turn off the TV and go for a walk." This statement was not posed as a question!

"Well, okay," I mumbled unenthusiastically as the ref cancelled an artistic slam-dunk with a call of travelling.

"You'll get more than enough basketball once the March Madness playoffs get underway," Anne added, trying to soften my disappointment at leaving an unfinished tied game.

Having played long ago on the Carleton College varsity team, I'm still semi-addicted to vicariously reliving those days by watching the pros and college talent of today. But on this particular warm, wind-free, sunny Sunday afternoon, my wife Anne, our dog Mele, and I set out for a stroll through the forest behind our house in Flagstaff, Arizona. We headed east on a well-beaten track, more or less contouring along the base of Elden, a steep-sided, two-thousand-foot-tall volcano (dacite lava dome) — an impressive backdrop for our home. I brought a digital camera to photograph a massive alligator juniper tree that we knew of along this path.

A mile plus later, there we were at the tree whose gnarly five-foot-wide trunk is purported to have lived through more years of history than our nation. After a bit of jockeying, I decided I'd found the right position for the perfect shot, only to discover that the camera's batteries were dead. In hind sight, this was an omen of what was yet to come. Death and the threat thereof were to be today's themes.

Rather than head back home, we decided to push on an extra half mile to revisit the site of the mid-1880s homestead of the Elden family, the mountain's namesake. The place includes a clearing where the Elden cabin once stood, and a nearby spring that was the source of their water, a critically valuable resource in arid Arizona. There is also a lone lonely grave, whose background story is a tragic tale of accidental death of the Eldens' young son.

Anne and I had visited this place several times before, but I'd never seen the spring flowing. I thought with our recent snowmelt, today might be the day to prove that Elden Spring was aptly named. Anne and Mele stayed to explore the cabin site while I hiked the thirty yards or so, out of sight, down into the streambed.

Surprise! Water was seeping from fissures along the base of the mountain, and gathering into a small but inviting flow. Someone had fashioned a crude channel that directed the flow into a holding tank. As I soaked in this refreshing scene, a red fox suddenly appeared, about twenty feet away, on the far side of the streambed. He came running directly toward me at top speed, squealing and yipping like the sounds of a small unhappy dog. *Anne heard this noise and assumed the sounds were from the dog of another nearby, though unseen, hiker.* I was under attack. I had no time to create a workable plan for evasive action. My sole thought was that the critter must be rabid because healthy foxes run away from humans, not at them.

Before I could take a single step in flight — hey, he was faster than I was anyway — he sank his teeth into the toe of my right sneaker, but apparently not into flesh as I felt no pain. I lifted and shook my leg until he fell free. His sharp pointed teeth left a row of parallel saliva-covered rips across the flimsy cloth of my sneaker's toe. Energized by an adrenalin rush, I managed to score a kick powerful enough to put him back on the other side of the streambed. Had it been a tied score in the last few seconds of football play, I could have kicked a game-winning fifty-yard field goal for the Carleton Knights!

With that kick, I lost my balance and staggered backwards into a small tree, snapping off dead branches as I fell. Weeks afterward, I still have angry-looking welts across my back from the fall. *Anne heard the snapping sounds and thought someone nearby was target-shooting.* By the time I was back on my feet, the furry attacker was bee-lining for me again. At the last second in a somewhat youthful athletic move, I spun sideways and managed to connect with a strong soccer-style kick before he could sink his teeth into me. This time he landed on my side of the streambed, unconscious. I saw blood-tinted froth bubbling from his mouth.

I scrambled away, shouting "Don't come down here!! Don't come down here!!!" *Anne heard my shouting, but couldn't understand the message.* At the cabin site I quickly gathered up Anne and Mele. "Let's get out of here!"

We jogged a ways down the path, and stopped briefly to catch our breath. My sixty-eight-year-old lungs were stressed by the fox encounter, age, and the thin air of our 7,000-foot elevation. Between gasps I gave Anne a short version of what had happened at the spring. As I talked, she and I — foolishly, in hindsight — explored my torn sneaker, with no concern about fox saliva wetting our hands. We then strode briskly home, warning other Sunday afternoon hikers away from Elden Spring.

I called Flagstaff's Animal Control Department. A cell-phone carrying person we had warned along the trail had already contacted them. An officer arrived at our door minutes later and asked me to accompany him and his colleague to the site of the attack. They were armed with ten-foot hollow fiberglass poles threaded with metal cable shaped into a loop that could be tightened around the neck of an out-of-control critter, from the relative safety of the pole's other end. I was armed with fear so palpable that I was sure that I could outrun any fox we might encounter.

I led them to the spring, lagging behind while giving voice and hand directions. Damned if the fox wasn't still there — bloodied mouth, conscious again, and about a hundred feet downstream from where he had attacked me. He charged madly as soon as he saw us. I cringed behind as the animal control professionals proved that they knew how to use the tool of their trade.

March 16: The opening round of March Madness starts tomorrow. Today, the results from the chemical test of the fox's brain arrived from a lab in Phoenix and confirmed what smart money would have bet on all along. Rabid!! More rabid than a U Conn fan. During our eight days of waiting for the results, Anne and I were oblivious to the fact that by handling my ripped sneaker, we had exposed ourselves to the rabies virus via fox saliva. When that was explained to us, as part of the lab report, we immediately began the series of anti-rabies shots.

March 30: We're down to the final four, and both Arizona teams have been eliminated. Rats! The better news is that the fourth anti-rabies shot will be administered at the Coconino County Health Clinic this afternoon. Shot five, the last of the series, will take place

in two more weeks. Thank goodness the shots are not the old infamously painful ones in the stomach, but rather today they are like the pinprick of a flu shot in the shoulder. At nearly $200 apiece, any significant pain will be to our pocketbook. But the experts tell us that the alternative, once the rabies virus has infected a human body, is almost certain death. We fancy that our lives are worth a couple thousand dollars!

April 1: In three days we'll know which teams will be the final two. No fooling. Anne has stopped chiding me for being a B-ball-watching couch potato. Instead, she joins me. The rabid fox incident has convinced us to live each day like it might be the last. We often wonder aloud how long this sobering effect will stay with us. We still take Mele on daily walks. A Doberman pinscher needs exercise! But we're now sticking to Flagstaff's paved residential streets. And I practice the non-political version of Teddy Roosevelt's sage advice. "Walk quietly and carry a big stick." My big stick is a four-foot piece of 2x2 hardwood. I simulate fox repelling by savagely batting pine cones as we stroll down our quiet neighborhood lanes. People watching from their houses may think I'm crazy, but there's a sound reason for this apparent madness.

This time of year, this year, March Madness came in two varieties. May future years bring only the B-ball type!

PELE
A Poem in Remembrance

From almost the day after our wedding, Anne and I have kept a Doberman pinscher as a house pet. These dogs have all been beloved family members. As noted animal behaviorist Konrad Lorenz has written, the sadness of keeping such an animal in the family is that humans almost always outlive the four-legged member. (Somewhat paraphrased, but you get the idea.) We've always assuaged our grief at losing a pet by finding a puppy replacement. I wrote the following in remembrance of Pele, the immediate predecessor of our current dog Mele.

> We found her during winter time,
> The short days dark and cold.
> She came to us a bouncy pup,
> Of barely six weeks old.
>
> That first night in our house kept brisk
> We quickly did discover
> That begging eyes and pleading whines
> Joined us beneath bed cover.

All family members need a name,
For each should be unique.
With Dobie's German ancestry,
She couldn't be Monique.

We searched our minds for something apt
A name we could admire.
And in the end we settled on
A label much like fire.

Pele, then, she did become …
The letter-count quite modest.
We had no soccer star in mind.
Our dog, Hawaiian *Goddess*.

A goddess should be bright you know,
And Pele proved this true.
Within a week of Anne's firm help,
Dog training she raced through.

Come, sit, and heel, and stay she learned
In the twinkling of an eye.
Then begged treats for her straight *As*.
Our Pele was not shy!

She quickly grew to be adult,
Sleek short hair, firm full chest.
But floppy ears of natural mode
Would keep her from breed's best.

Though of a class oft said to act
Aggressive! Vicious! Mean!
Our Pele never hurt a flea
Nor caused a public scene.

She loved all people, young and old.
She even loved our cat.
Soon, Pele weighed some eighty pounds.
Twas out of bed … to dog mat.

She traveled with us near and far
Unless the law said no.
She loved to walk, or run, or ride.
Just anywhere, she'd go.

'Long side our horses, in ski tracks
She moved as light as feather.
She didn't mind rain, sleet, or snow
Pure joy tuned out bad weather.

Then came the family motor home,
Wisconsin trips, back east.
She sniffed her way from Flag to lake,
The miles a scented feast.

There at the lake we soon did learn
With smarts she had one battle.
In water deeper than her legs,
She failed the test, dog paddle.

She'd sit and watch, sprawl on the dock,
As Anne and I swam by.
Still, when the pontoon boat went out
To the deck she'd fly.

The time passed much too fast, and soon
We all were nine years older.
Pele slowed, as did we all,
Her head upon a shoulder.

The saddest truth of Dobie pets,
    For long-lived human men
Is that this breed is rarely seen
    To live beyond year ten.

The final night, the time that
    We'd prepared for, full of dread.
We did what love told our sad hearts …
    Had Pele in our bed.

Thus, she slept full circle there,
    Her first and her last hours.
Her ashes now reminders dear.
    They fertilize our flowers.

A FUNNY THING HAPPENED AT THIS FUNERAL

IT'S BEEN MY observation that the words *funny* and *funeral* don't often appear in the same simple declarative sentence. But they perfectly mate to describe my personal experience at a funeral I attended.

I'm not particularly fond of funerals. I've always preferred to spend quality time with people who are very much alive. But as I and my covey of family and closest friends age into and beyond the sexagenarian decade, funerals are an increasingly common reason for a gathering. And so it was that I recently set out on a journey to bid adieu to yet another loved one.

With quickly packed suitcase in tow, I caught a flight that transported me over five states and across two time zones, to where an Avis car-rental agent awaited my signature. Three hours later, I parked on a grassy glade adjacent to a small-town church where the ceremony would transpire.

I was early. The only others present were a husband-and-wife mortician team, under whose guidance funeral arrangements had been made and were now in the final stages of being carried out. As I entered, they were positioning bouquets of flowers about the vestibule. A book for attendees to sign sat open to page one on a small table near the entrance door. Across the room, the deceased lay in an open casket next to double-door access into the sanctuary where the formal funeral service would take place. The casket was perched atop a cart that would soon be wheeled into a front-and-center position for the pastor-led ceremony.

I introduced myself and described my relationship to the deceased. As they busied themselves with final arrangements in the vestibule, I said my silent last goodbye to my dear friend. The lid of the casket was in two sections — one open so viewers would see the deceased from the waist up. The adult male body looked incredibly life-like, and was dressed as if planning to attend a normal Sunday morning service, as he had for so many years at this church. Beneath an earth-tone suit, a starched white shirt was cinched at his neck by a flawlessly arranged tie.

Soon others would begin arriving. Suitcase in hand, I retreated to the men's room to change from comfy travel attire into conservative matched slacks and sport coat, a white shirt, and my funeral-service tie. Dad had long before trained me in the art of creating a Windsor knot. But today I was not mastering the sequence of over, around, across and through — or was it across, over, around and through. Neither sequence resulted in an attractive knot. Nerves? Lack of recent practice? Whatever. After several failed attempts, frustrated and embarrassed, I returned to the vestibule for help.

Lady mortician was busy over the casket — perhaps a last minute inspection to assure that clothing of the deceased had not become rumpled during transport from mortuary to church. I approached silently and tapped her shoulder.

"Could you help me with my necktie?" I timidly asked in muted voice.

She turned and then smiled when I presented her with the object of my frustration. She turned back to the deceased and ran an open hand down his necktie in a final smoothing gesture.

Then, looking again at me, "Of course," she said, face adorned with the pleasant but not frivolous smile of a mortician. "But you'll have to lie completely still in a supine position." I would laugh later, and frequently, during the years since then.

She and I used an empty pew for my support as she deftly created the most perfect Windsor knot I have ever sported. I have never since tried to tie a Windsor knot, or any other traditional necktie intertwining concoction. Clip-on works well.

PARTS OF SPEECH

Written for Marlowe "Red" Severson, the ninth-grade English teacher who helped inspired my enjoyment of writing.

When prose or poetry wants action,
Vibrant verbs provide the traction.

If an object needs a name,
Some fine noun enters the game.

Perhaps a noun is too specific?
Some pronoun would be terrific.

All conjunctions are connective,
And are used to be reflective.

If a writing seems too dry,
Adjectives can make it fly.

Adverbs now and then are timely,
And their sounds sing out sublimely.

Prepositions are phrase intros,
Whose word tasks are added infos.

If writing cries for keen attention,
Add interjection intervention!

Parts of speech are well worth knowing,
If your writings you'll be showing.

ORGANIZED RELIGION AND ME

AS I AGE, I find my mind increasingly wandering back across the decades, reliving times and places and events that shaped and reshaped me into whatever I am today. One such time trip transports me to the doorstep of a staunchly God-fearing Methodist boy who evolved into an even stauncher atheist as an adult. (Or is it agnostic? There are so many nuanced shades of both atheist and agnostic and other god-related positions that a definitive answer is unlikely to satisfy all readers. I'll call myself an atheist for this essay.) Many recent news stories and books report that a secular life is increasingly popular in America. Whether others traveled a path parallel to mine in their departure from organized religion, I know not. Nonetheless, describing my journey may resonate with some — and motivate others to rethink their position on religion. Perhaps some of today's cadre of aging Baby Boomers will appreciate the story of a near age contemporary who was born as USA involvement in WWII was getting underway.

    I was raised in a fairly isolated west-central Minnesota farm-country town, with a population of about one thousand human souls. Surnames ending in *-son* and *-ski* were common. The people were predominantly second- or third-generation descendants of northern and northwestern European immigrant stock. Typical skin color varied seasonally from a pasty white during long cold winter months to farmer's-tan brown (i.e., for the arms and necks; the remaining skin stayed a shade of pasty white) during hot and humid sunny summers.

Superficially, we were all a homogenous lot. However, as I grew from my sheltered single-digit years into a teenager and beyond, I came to realize that similar outward appearances and shared ancestry can mask very different and sometimes divisive internal sets of values and beliefs. To wit, religion: Whereas my home town was populated by Caucasian Christians, their interpretations and practices of Christianity were anything but uniform, and often seemed to be as fickle and stormy as the Midwestern weather.

My awareness of my family's brand of Christianity began when I was old enough to recognize the meanings of words and their messages as relayed by subject-verb-predicate sentences. I suppose my first encounter may have begun earlier, if it's possible for a fetus to absorb its host mother's thoughts through amniotic fluid.

I was an offspring of parents thoroughly steeped in the beliefs and practices of the Methodist Church. Bible-toting founders John Wesley and his brother Charles of the eighteenth century were family heroes. My formal Methodist indoctrination began with the figurative baby steps required to become an official member of that church.

First came baptism at age one according to "Childhood Memories," a book that Mother compiled and eventually passed along to me. A little water on the head and a few words by the pastor sealed that deal. I was then a thirty pounder — probably quite a squirmy armful for Mother to hold as pastor did his splashy deed. I certainly had no idea how what was transpiring might impact my future life. If this ritual was meant to wash away original sin, pastor might have been more effective had he applied his cleansing water to the probable contents of my diaper!

Our family attended Sunday church services regularly. Only serious illness or travel (rare in family-farm country, where animals require daily human-provided care) were acceptable excuses for absence. By the time I had aged to year seven, or maybe it was only six or as much as eight, I was directed to sit erect and attentive on an uncomfortable hardwood pew during each Sunday morning service. In younger years, I slept through sermons with my head resting on Mother's lap. But now my age-contemporary soon-to-be church members and I were instructed to take notes and write a one-page report on the meaning and importance of the Pastor's message. I don't remember if my reports were read, edited, critiqued, or returned to me. But they were religiously (pun intended) recorded. Each report earned a gold star on a time-line chart kept by a church elder. In hind sight, it's transparent that the report evaluations mostly reflected the church's desire for new members. We all scored perfect gold-star records!

At some point at about this age, we recruits were immersed in a lesson about alcoholic beverages, the consumption of which was strictly forbidden by Methodist Church edict. A series of lectures for this part of membership training was followed by a color film depicting how consumption of alcohol attacks the human brain — moving images used to support words full of dire warnings. This may have caught our attention simply as the first color movie most of us kids had seen. Today, all these decades later, I retain a vivid mental image of the colorful climactic scene in which the cross-section of a man's brain is shown to be in an advanced stage of rot due to his taste for beer. Ugly and scary! The agent of decay was specifically beer, although wine would have been equally appropriate; Methodist Communion served up non-fermented grape juice. A bit of firm gray healthy brain was included in the sobering scene so we could compare.

An honest physician would have been properly skeptical. But as a young uncritical viewer I told myself that I certainly would avoid booze throughout my life. Yes, this naïve child swallowed the anti-alcohol lesson. When asked to do so on that day, my fellow inductees and I signed on a dotted line thereby promising — along with many other clearly stated requirements that go with being a Methodist — to never ever drink alcohol. We were forthwith deemed worthy of membership into the Methodist Church. Graduation! A King James Bible came as a gift. I probably even felt a bit of pride!!

Confirmation class, proudly holding bibles. Author second from left.

But shortly thereafter, my maturing mind roamed beyond church-defined boundaries and began to identify and critique confusing and conflicting ideas and practices in Methodist membership training. Though I didn't know how to evaluate these feelings at the time, I was experiencing the replacement of naiveté with reason — faith confronted by fact. It would have been so easy to passively continue believing information I was spoon fed by the church, but ...

A simple thought continued running through my awakening mind. Since all of the townspeople were Christians, why were there so many different churches? Why didn't my family and my school friends and their families gather under one large inclusive roof as followers of Jesus' teachings? Instead, town folks were spread across our village at multiple places of worship, each with a different name.

Curiosity prompted me, bare-foot and inquisitive, to walk the streets while I made notes and counted. There were five churches

— Catholic, Episcopal, Lutheran, Methodist, and Presbyterian, in alphabetical order. Catholic also came first in church size and steeple-reaching-for-heaven architectural grandeur. At the other end of the structure-appeal scale, there was a sixth, short-lived denomination called Holy Rollers. These practitioners met in a small rectangular cement-block building positioned on a hillside such that the church lay half underground. The place could have been mistaken for a potato cellar. That sanctuary of Jesus rolled away to some never-explained end within a year or two of appearing — perhaps for lack of membership? When a thousand souls are divvied up among five (or six) churches, membership numbers for a single sect are not large, even when farm families from the surrounding countryside are counted among the practitioners.

As newly discovered facts continued to chip away at my naiveté about religion, reasons for the multiplicity of churches increasingly came into focus. Some divisive practices between the sects seemed trivial if not downright silly, such as Methodists using the word *trespasses* where Presbyterians said *debts* in The Lord's Prayer. I first heard the clashing tonal dissidence of these words spoken simultaneously at a rare joint Christmas-season gathering. When I asked my parents why there were different words, they explained it as "customary." I was left with the impression that such customs weren't meant to be questioned, at least not by an inexperienced youth like me.

Seemingly more substantial in the not-to-be-questioned use of language, I learned from school mates that much of the Catholic Church service was spoken in a strange-sounding foreign tongue — something called Latin. Latin, I pondered. What the heck is that? So far as I knew, English was the country's language — the only language I had ever heard at that point in my life. Catholic school friends explained that translations from Latin to English were provided, so they would know what was being said and what was expected of them.

I, however, remained puzzled. The language for a church service is just a choice, I reasoned. It's not really important so long as the church's message is conveyed, right? We're all talking about the same inspirational historical figure and learning to uniformly follow his teachings, aren't we? Well aren't we!?

Not so, I learned as I reached the age when girls suddenly became desirables rather than pariahs. This budding attraction led me to a first date (and follow-up dates) with someone who happened to be Catholic. I didn't think about her religion when I invited her to the Roxie. We enjoyed going to movies and sharing popcorn. We were wowed by something as simple as holding hands. We eventually experienced a few chaste kisses. But when it became obvious that ours was not a one-time flirtation, Dad drew me aside for a stern man-to-man (man-to-boy) lecture about what was wrong with the Catholic version of Christianity.

Bottom line: he ordered me to stop dating that girl solely because she was Catholic. "What? Whoa!" I silently shouted. He said that when a non-Catholic marries a Catholic, he (or she) is required to formally join the Catholic Church and disavow any other church membership. Dad wasn't about to lose a Methodist to the Catholic faith — most certainly not one of his own offspring and his only son. I was the sole vessel he was molding to carry on the family name, and I should definitely do so as a Methodist.

"Wow! Kinda dumb" I thought, especially since the word marriage was not in my youthful vocabulary!! I obeyed Dad, of course, while increasingly wondering what exactly Christianity was. As the odds would have it, there were plenty of interesting non-Catholic girls around to help me enjoy the company of the opposite sex without Dad's hex. A held hand is a held hand, Catholic or not. I discovered that non-Catholic kissable lips meshed fine with mine. And what kid doesn't like popcorn?!

From an accidentally overheard conversation, I came to realize that Dad's distaste for Catholicism ran emotionally deep and bitter. In a nutshell, he thought it totally unfair that if he sinned in the eyes of his church, he had to wallow in guilt, essentially forever I guess, until the freeing that comes with death took over. In contrast, as I heard him say to one of his fellow non-Catholics, "Gosh all fish hooks, Joe! All a Catholic sinner has to do is go to confession, recite Hail Mary the priest-ordered number of times, and presto the sin-list slate is wiped clean. It ain't fair." He had a point there, I thought.

Dad had a solid Methodist reason for feeling the guilt of a sinner.

More than once, I saw him drinking cold beer on a hot summer day when he thought no one was looking. I wondered if he had ever been asked to watch an anti-alcohol movie during his membership training. I wasn't about to ask him that question, but if the answer had been yes, he surely was almost drowning in an ocean of boozy guilt. Yet, I noted that Dad's brain never atrophied from his surreptitious swigs. He was a bright and creative man, as a high school graduate. He taught me many useful day-to-day practical skills during my early years. Back then I figured I would be plenty happy to grow up to be just like him. I am still able to operate and repair a variety of pre-computer machines. I can capably saw boards, drive wood screws, and pound nails. As a career field geologist, I've even needed to repair a leaking car tire in the outback. And like Dad, my adult taste for alcoholic beverages has not impacted my brain to impair these talents.

As the 1940s passed into the next decade, I recognized more examples of how a town full of nominally love-thy-neighbor-as-thyself Christians was in fact a collection of clashing Catholics, Lutherans, Methodists, Presbyterians, and Episcopalians. I recall no fist fights, but I remember word duels, spoken and silent, as each denomination operated in the certainty that its brand of religion had the correct answer to whatever the faith-related question might be. This religion thing was getting more and more confusing for me. And for my age contemporaries too, I suppose, although we rarely talked about it. We just carried on, in the comfort zone of each family's church training. We were unaware of most adult issues, and too entertainment-centered (let's play pump pump pull away, or go swimming or fishing or sledding) to argue about such stuff. Some of us were starting to recognize widening cracks in the Christian foundations of our town, though.

Then at age fifteen a clear window opened, through which I discovered a broad fresh view of religion and infinite other topics. By unexpected chance I was uprooted from the narrow confines of my farm-country hometown and transplanted into an expansive multifaceted academic world. Fate whisked me away (a separate long story) to a boarding school in New England where my understanding of religion, and other topics, developed into increasingly mature and often multiple answers for questions that had been inadequately explored and explained in small-town Minnesota.

Somewhat ironically, I excelled at Latin in prep school. In fact, I became so proficient in this written, read, but seldom spoken language that by year three I was invited to represent our school of pointy-headed preppies at a Latin language contest sponsored by Harvard University in nearby Cambridge, Massachusetts. By then, I believed I could have written original Latin Catholic liturgy, to say nothing about translating it for my hometown contemporaries who might need wordsmith help.

In addition to Latin, I enrolled in a course called Comparative Religions and shared what I learned there with Mother and Dad via the U.S. Postal Service. From the beginning of this cursive conversation, my letters home triggered replies replete with disbelief of my statements, eventually followed by scorn amid a continuously growing concern that their son was "going astray." Our back-and-forth exchanges, basically penned mini debates, came to an abrupt halt with my letter pointing out that far more people on Earth are members of religions other than Christianity.

I guess that fact stunned Mother and Dad into silence. I was saying that their cloistered view of religion was fallible — that Christianity is just one brand of the many religions practiced on planet Earth, and not the most populated one at that. I imagine they didn't want to admit so. And their only son was the conveyor of such pain-inducing information. Expanding one's knowledge can sometimes be an upsetting, though always useful, experience.

After that, our views of religion and its role in one's life increasingly diverged, from my prep school years, across undergraduate college days, and beyond through a graduate-school education. By the time a PhD was in hand, Dad's openly voiced opinion of me was, "You used to be a nice, considerate, and grateful Methodist person." I also learned that my parents' advice to fellow hometown adults was "If your son is ever offered a chance to attend a prep school like our son did, don't let him go. If you do, you'll lose him."

It hurt to hear those and similar thoughts spill so easily from Mother and Dad's mouths. And all over something that is in theory a unifying, understanding, and love-filled institution: organized religion. As I advanced into adulthood, my fundamental core human values were, and are still, products of my sheltered early years; they just lack the narrow constraints of Methodism. I am a practitioner of the Golden Rule, but a version of that rule without religion-defined boundaries. Throughout the period beyond the event of my Methodist membership, those life values grew to encompass a much broader perspective, one that recognizes the valid role of diversity among peoples and their contrasting cultures worldwide. I evolved into a Golden-Rule-Guided atheist. By the way, if anyone tells you that the Golden Rule is an original Christian concept, tell them to do some research.

Many people have evolved through a radically and perhaps similarly changing view of religion. According to recently published national polls, an increasing number of other Americans have also left their churches for a secular life, or they never were part of an organized religion. Why has religion lost so much of its appeal? This goes far beyond being a good Methodist or not. The exodus from today's religions began centuries ago, and accelerated when emerging science began to explore some of the central existential questions.

For me and many others, science provides explanations for most natural phenomena and through observation and experimentation will continue to expand such knowledge. By contrast, many religions persist in an anti-science stance, or at a minimum refuse to accept scientific findings way beyond the limit of reason and reasonableness. This is faith promoting ignorance. For example, in spite of overwhelming accumulated evidence, it took Catholicism exceptionally long to admit that Earth is not the center of our solar system! Along similar anti-science thinking, recent polls indicate that more than fifty percent of our fellow citizens don't believe in evolution. A similarly large group thinks the age of the Earth is the biblical figure of around six thousand years. And, wow, a Flat Earth Society still persists?! And on and on. Friction between faith-based belief and demonstrable fact creates rather heated discussions and may never find rational, or at least middle ground. But why rely on faith where scientific experimentation offers so many accurate answers?

In addition to my attachment to science, I've been driven off the faith-based path in life because many religions are divisive, rather than uniting people in a common goal to better educate and comfort all humankind, even within a single religion such as Christianity — and as recent world events make clear to those who listen read and reason, within Islam too.

Organized religions are, well, organizations. They have charters. They have rules. They are hierarchical. They run recruiting programs. They have rigid requirements for membership. They own property. They are businesses — tax-free businesses. Many have amassed great wealth along the way, rather than unselfishly and equally sharing with the less fortunate, who they claim to represent and champion. And each flavor of these faith-based business organizations claims to be the tastiest, the one with the most satisfactorily correct menu of answers to life's puzzling questions.

In addition, religions often pursue their agendas through political action, ignoring the notion of separation between church and state. Politicians pander to religions by justifying governing decisions with such statements as "God told me to run for this office. God told me to vote this way." Et cetera. These people ignore the fact that any god is a creation of a human mind; thus in reality the pontificating politicians are telling themselves what to do, and throwing the blame, or credit, on god. Their mention of god is simply a lofty-sounding way to avoid personal responsibility.

Many religions also are exclusive and selective in terms of human relations. Looking back at another personal experience, the Methodist Church immediately dismissed a popular young female Pastor in my hometown when the fact that she is lesbian became public. This is not an exemplary action of the sisterly/brotherly love that Christianity claims to espouse, I think.

I have concluded that organized religion — in spite of ethical short comings, inter- and intra-sect foibles and institutional differences — generally has been able to flourish for millennia because many humans live with such a constant level of fear and uncertainty that they all too readily succumb to the promises of faith over the facts of reason. I suppose the ultimate fear may be that of death. Insofar as religion can help ease this fear for believers, it serves a soothing purpose.

I respect those who find strength, comfort, meaning, and purpose through faith. But I believe that the practices of religion should be kept separate from those of politics and science. I'm as comfortable with my science-based secular lifestyle as you may be with your religion. Let's stay friends. But as we contemplate our contrasting views on the meaning and mechanics of human life, we should, in the current popular vernacular of the cognoscenti *have that conversation* — a conversation that goes beyond simply believing something when demonstrable facts show an alternative reality.

As their contributions to such a conversation, today's Baby Boomers may be mentally traversing a critical threshold between continuing plans for lively enjoyment and nascent plans for … well, for the end. As a just-pre-boomer-aged person, I identify with the BB demographic. As a professional educated in geology, I also identify with the fact that the presence of humans on a planet that has been around for 4.6 billion years is truly a wee blink of the eye — that is, of the eye that sees beyond the biblical version of our planet's lifespan. I keep that fact in mind as I contemplate the approach of my death. For me, the enormity of geologic time is humbling. By comparison, my seven or more decades on Earth will be, well, pretty unimportant. It's been an exhilarating and perhaps even a bit of a productive trip, and I'm okay with the coming end without trying to convince myself that that end is the beginning of an eternal blissful existence in some ethereal make-believe realm.

A VERY BELATED CONFESSION AND APOLOGY

I WAS RAISED by very loyal and strict Methodist parents. They saw to it that I was baptized into their church at age one, and then went through proper Methodist training to become an official member of that Christian institution by the time I was barely into my double-digit years.

Though I am no longer a practicing Methodist, one church-taught trait that I believe is still part of my character is the practice of the Golden Rule — *Do Unto Others As You Would Have Them Do Unto You,* or some other combination of words that expresses the same notion.

So here I am today to confess my breaking of that rule, some fifty-three years after the fact. I am writing this essay because I have not yet been able to erase my dirty deed from memory. Feelings of guilt and shame pop up at seemingly random times, and in so doing continue to haunt the recesses of my consciousness, including the semi-conscious state of sleep. And as I age, even sleep is becoming an increasingly precious commodity of daily life. Perhaps a formal and very public airing of my sin will provide desired relief? I suspect that Mark Twain would have some appropriate words to describe and perhaps explain my dilemma, if only I could find the proper paragraph in his vast published writings.

Well, here's the story. And it is true, to the best of my memory. In fact, this entire essay is an accurate reporting of my memory.

When I was a student at Carleton College in Northfield, Minnesota, I spent considerable time studying in the carrels of the library. These one-student desks sprinkled throughout the stacks of book collections were quiet places, which helped one concentrate without the typical dormitory distractions. On one such study binge, my carrel came with a textbook that I would soon need to buy. It was an expensive book. I was a scholarship boy working my way through college. I suppose an absent-minded fellow student simply walked away empty handed, his mind filled with just-learned information needed for some exam.

I opened the book and saw a name penned in the upper right corner of the first page. I didn't know this person.

I don't remember the thoughts that likely crossed my mind during the next few moments. But I do remember neatly cutting away the autographed page corner. I then added his to my pile of textbooks and walked back to my dorm.

The next day I was at that same carrel, studying for some upcoming test or quiz, when a student walked up and asked if I had seen his book there. So now, reader, you can see the folly of my returning to the same carrel. Had I only been thinking logically, I would have expected this classmate to return to where he last had his book in hand. But I liked that particular carrel, because it was at a window with a relaxing view across a grassy knoll to Lyman Lakes. This was welcome visual relief between binges of fine-print reading.

Well, my negative answer was an out-and-out lie, albeit a safe one in the sense that the purloined book was back in my dorm room. And this is the lie still embedded in the deep contorted recesses of my cranial memory bank. You may laugh, reader, but this is true. Had I been raised a Catholic, confessed this sin to a priest, and voiced his prescribed number of Hail Marys, would I have erased the dirty deed from my memory. I think not.

Today, finally, I would very much like to personally confess and apologize to my victim. But I don't know his name or the subject matter of his book. Maybe he is alive and will read this essay. If so, please please contact me. Today's world events and political shenanigans are enough daily negatives, without adding my continuing regret of stealing your book and lying to you.

I suppose I might find some solace for my burden of guilt by rereading the antics of Twain's Huckleberry Finn and Tom Sawyer. Perhaps it's time to revisit my legally purchased collection of Twain's writings.

LIMERICK-LUBRICATED TRANSITION TIME AGAIN

A normally placid friend Pam
On trips would become quite the ham
When asked 'bout this change
Her voice became strange
And her acting got worse than raw spam

A linguist and huntsman named Paul
Will make carnivores of us all
While we sit and hope
He spots with his scope
Looking for game he can maul

And then there's the sportsman named Jim
Who'll challenge an elk on a whim
When asked why he does it
He says just because it
Enhances his home's inner trim

And finally let's not forget Sue
Any one from the tasty Sue stew
It you want one of them
Just call out the name
If all answer you'll have quite a crew

A FIELD-WORK ADVENTURE IN HAWAII

IN 1975, KEITH Howard, Mel Beeson, and I (all U.S. Geological Survey geologists) had a fieldwork adventure on the island of Molokai, Hawaii, that none of us will ever forget. We were headquartered in Menlo Park, California, at that time. Mel was in the midst of studying the chemistry of the sixteen hundred-foot-thick section of lava flows exposed along the foot trail that descends to Father Damien's well-known leper colony on the Kalaupapa Peninsula of Molokai. I was mapping volcanic rocks here and there in California. Keith was plugged into the USGS program of Astrogeologic Studies. Somehow he convinced his money managers that one could learn a lot about the geology of Mars by studying the caldera of East Molokai Volcano. The three of us ... young, enthusiastic, and in search of adventure ... teamed up to do so.

A helicopter ferried us and our equipment into this very remote rainforest area. The pilot assured us that he would pick us up three weeks later. As our last glimpse of "civilization" for those coming weeks choppered out of sight, we made camp, filled with energy and grand expectations of improving the pioneering geologic mapping done in the 1940s by Harold Stearns and Gordon Macdonald.

We began in Wailau Valley, a deep north-flowing drainage carved into the east flank of the volcano. We quickly discovered that lush tropical vegetation hid virtually all bedrock. Desperate to put our geology picks to use, we shed our clothing and swam streams to the few rocks that peeked through greenery. By day eight of nude fieldwork, we were very discouraged by the paucity of real rocks. And almost worse, by then we were completely bummed out by our victuals.

Keith had purchased a pallet of surplus military K-rations, as our sole source of nourishment. They were lightweight and highly caloric, and the price was right. But with only four different meals, we soon ate solely to stay alive. Adventuresome Keith tried snails from Wailau Stream and raw taro root. Ugggh! Smart Keith was a one-trial learner and went back to K-rations.

Hoping for better outcrops, we headed west into Pelekunu, a deep valley eroded across the caldera. Getting there was a two-day seemingly life-threatening adventure. What we had been told would be a well-marked trail, definitely wasn't. Nonetheless we found Malihini Cave, the bedroom target for our first night. We slept outside in the rain though, rather than on a cave floor covered ankle-deep in goat poop. Next day we crested three thousand-foot-tall razor-back drainage-divide Kolo Ridge, and stumbled more than walked down to a USGS stream-gauging-station shack where we found a meal's worth of Spam … Yummy!!!

Field traverses in Pelekunu Valley verified what we had discovered on the first day in Wailau. Most of the landscape was covered by ferns and grasses and bushes and trees. But along some stream banks we found outcrops of dike swarms and hydrothermally altered lava, presumably parts of the guts of the caldera. Other enticing outcrops stared down at us from inaccessible tall cliffs.

And of course at one of the planet's wettest places, it rained and rained and then rained some more. We entertained ourselves during down times by carving Hawaiian flutes from sections of bamboo and trying to make music. For variety, we gathered the pea-sized shiny off-white seeds (called Job's Tears) of a tall grass and strung them into attractive necklaces. Thirty-four years later, I still have my Job-Tear creations and am wearing one of those necklaces as I type these words. But with each passing Pelekunu day, we were getting sicker and sicker and sicker of K-rations.

Flutists Duff (left) and Keith.

In semi-desperation for dietary variety, Keith and I went on the bare-handed hunt for one of the many feral pigs that thrive in Hawaiian rainforests. We caught one, about a thirty pounder. The three of us gathered, catch in hand, and salivated until we realized that we didn't have the heart to kill the little porker. The fact that piglet was crawling with lice was another deterrent to slaughter and feast.

Keith (left) piglet and Duff.

It was to be K-rations to the end, other than the fruit of a banana tree we found near camp.

Mel with Fresh Bananas.

February 25: Our escape helicopter arrived on schedule and deposited us at the Molokai Airport. A wiki-wiki cab took us to a hotel in Kaunakakai, the island's main town. My wife Anne, who normally is terrified to even get near an airplane, had flown in from the mainland to greet me. I paused long enough to plant a cursory kiss. Then we all headed to the nearest café, where Keith, Mel, and I overate. Next morning, as Anne and I awoke in a warm embrace, my first words were, "I've been dreaming about an apple turnover." Later that morning, back at the café, Keith, Mel, and I ate two full breakfasts each. To this day, Anne likes to teasingly remind me of how much more interested I was in food, than in her, during our Kaunakakai reunion.

MY ROLE IN A REVOLUTION
A Tale of Tectonic Shift

A note of explanation to earth scientists writ large, friends, and other readers. The following essay generalizes and simplifies complex concepts and hypotheses. My reason for writing the piece is to inform how my life as a geologist was molded and then substantially remolded by living across a timeline when first-order progress was attained in geologists' understanding of planet Earth. I think this experience was somewhat akin to having lived when Homo sapiens discovered that Earth is not flat, or when scientists came to realize that Earth is just one of many bodies that are gravitationally captive as subsidiaries to our Sun.

WHEN THE WORD *revolution* enters a conversation, the topic generally is about the politics of governing some piece of real estate called a country. My country has been (relatively) stable during my lifetime to date. But my life-long profession, geology, experienced a major revolution in its understanding of how the rocky outer layer of our planet — called the crust or lithosphere by geologists — changes shape and geographic position.

This revolution happened shortly after I had been taught the "old story" on my way to earning a 1963 BA in geology. Back then gospel was that crust underwent episodes of moving up and down, to form mountains and valleys of various sizes and shapes; but never ever did it migrate sideways more than just enough to allow such ups and downs to occur.

Back then and today, deformation of Earth's crust, that brittle miles-thick rind upon which we humans reside, was and is described by the term *tectonics* or *tectonism*. By the time I finished graduate school with a 1967 PhD in hand, the word *plate* became part of the term, as in *plate tectonics*, in recognition that Earth's crust consists of a dozen or so large pieces, which through geologic time have moved and will continue to move vast horizontal distances relative to each other. Bumping, grinding, and pulling apart at the edges of these plate-like pieces give rise to Earth's mountains and valleys. The ups and downs of the "old story" are basically second-order results. This discovery was truly a revolution for interpreting crust's past geologic history and in foreseeing its possibilities for future behavior.

A variety of newly developed techniques to map the shape and ages of Earth's crust fueled this geologic revolution. Detailed surveys of ocean floors discovered hitherto unknown long sinuous mountain chains (e.g. Mid-Atlantic Ridge and East Pacific Rise) where most of Earth's active volcanoes are located. Simultaneously, new techniques for calculating numerical ages of volcanic rocks showed that these ocean-floor lavas are successively older with increasing distance from the sea-floor ridges. Ergo, the sea floor moves away from the ridges and eventually this conveyor-belt material plunges deeply back into Earth where it creates new magma for volcanic eruptions. And all of these plate motions play out in a background of earthquakes, mostly around plate edges.

As with revolutions of all varieties, not all geologist *Homo sapiens* were pleased with this fundamental change about Earth's tectonism. The interpretations/explanations described in much of the pre-revolution published research were suddenly brought into question. But within a few years, with repeated testing of the concepts attributed to *global plate tectonics,* the new model of Earth prevailed.

As a side issue, I've noticed that many non-geologist news reporters have adopted the term *tectonic* to describe large noteworthy shifts in a variety of daily-life events. But I digress.

During the turmoil of the ongoing tectonic shift in the accepted geology paradigm, I happened to be on the staff at the Hawaiian Volcano Observatory where a long-lived eruption was underway. For several weeks, a lake of molten basalt sloshed sluggishly about in a crater on the flank of Kilauea Volcano. Quenched by contact with relatively cool atmosphere, the surface of the lake was veneered with a thin solid crust. And having become familiar with the revolution underway in my profession, I recognized that this crust consisted of an ever-evolving interacting arrangement of plates whose motions mimicked those of Earth's tectonic plates. For readers with a geologic vocabulary, the lava lake was veneered by a mesmerizing surface decorated with small-scale subduction zones, mid-oceanic spreading centers, and transform faults.

Two spreading centers connected by a right-lateral transform fault. Zone of white melt is about one meter wide, before quenching to solid black crust.

Daredevil geologist discovers what happens when he straddles a transform fault.

I documented this action with still and motion pictures. Meanwhile, geology professors worldwide had become almost desperate for teaching aids that could readily and clearly illustrate global plate tectonics for their students. The lava-lake version helped fill that teaching-tool void. I sold hundreds of copies of the movie and slides.

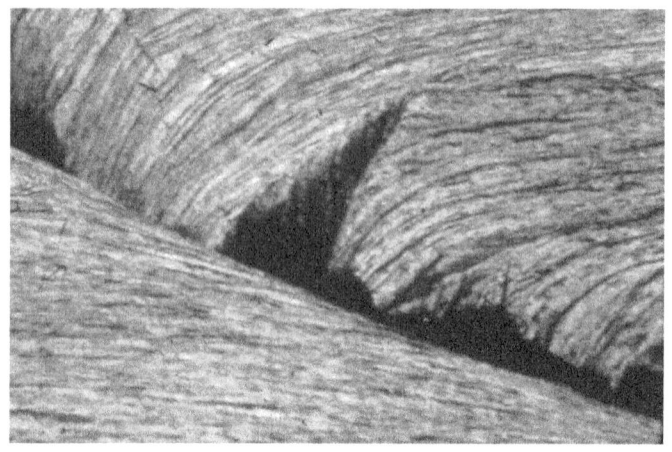

Subduction zone, where crust on the left plunges beneath crust on the right.

Can this geologist run faster than the rate of subduction?

And that, readers, was my role in the greatest revolution to roil geology during the past several human generations. No guns needed. Just eyes and ideas! How lucky I was to be where I was as the revolution played out. It seems that serendipity walked up and slapped me smack across the face.

For anyone who might want to follow up with formal publications:

Wendell Duffield, 1972, A naturally occurring model of global plate tectonics: *Journal of Geophysical Research*, v. 77, no. 14, p. 2543-2555.

Wendell Duffield, 1972, Kilauea Volcano provides a model for plate tectonics: *Geotimes*, v. 17, no. 4, p. 19-21

SERENDIPITY AND SCIENCE

Serendipity: noun; The faculty of finding valuable or agreeable things not sought for.

IN MARCH OF 1982 a volcano name El Chichon, in the Mexican state of Chiapas, erupted violently. The top of the mountain was blown away, and mingled with newly erupted lava, came to rest as thick deposits of shattered rock and pumice around the volcano's base, gradually thinning out into the surrounding hilly forest. Francisco Leon, a town at the base of the volcano, was destroyed. Hundreds of residents there and at ranchos scattered across the surrounding terrain were killed. The newly formed hot and seething explosion crater, hundreds of feet deep, quickly hosted a few small ponds of acrid water, fed by the region's rainfall … nearly two hundred inches per year.

El Chichon Volcano, before and just after the 1982 eruption.

Several weeks later, when the volcano's recent rage seemed safely spent, the Mexican Government invited U.S. Geological Survey (USGS) volcanologists Bob Tilling and me to visit the area and offer our assessment of the character of the eruption and of what the follow-up in coming weeks if not years might entail. We worked with Mexican geologist counterparts, and were supported by two government helicopters. Renewed road access did not yet exist.

Volcanoes generally occur in clusters, as seen for example in the San Francisco Volcanic Field of northern Arizona, or in long chains such as the Cascade Volcanic Range of California through Washington State and into Canada. El Chichon, however, is a solitary volcano within a mountainous region cloaked with a tropical rain forest. Perhaps because of its remote location and difficult access, geologists didn't recognize El Chichon as a volcano until the early 1900s. However, the nearby native population may have suspected that a powerful force of nature lay within this one mountain, which hosted warm stinking fumaroles and hot springs.

The name *El Chichon* also carries an unusual story. Chichonal is a variety of tree that thrives on the slopes of the volcano and whose rather lumpy fruit was a food staple for the surrounding native population. The Spanish word *chichon* is also used to describe the kind of lump one can grow on a strongly bumped head. Males being males, our counterpart colleagues were also happy to share with us that in Mexico chichon is slang for a female breast. My knowledge of Spanish suggests that "¡Que chichones!" translates to "What boobs!" But I digress.

During the eruption, a thick tongue of pyroclastic debris flowed down a drainage channel on the flank of El Chichon and created a dam across the Magdalena River as the hot rocky stuff accumulated there. The Magdalena flows along about half of the volcano's base on a sinuous path through the rain forest. A large lake quickly formed behind the dam in this land of rain rain and more rain. At its maximum size, the lake submerged what evidence was left of the town Francisco Leon, several miles upstream of the dam. Because the lake bottom consisted of erupted rocks still several hundred degrees Fahrenheit, the lake-water temperature quickly rose to near boiling. The continuous upstream input of cool rain runoff was barely sufficient to suppress boiling.

The lake had topped its dam and quickly drained days before Bob and I arrived. We saw its high-water shorelines etched into hillsides and a broad U-shaped breach where the dam had failed and had been eroded during draining. Mexican authorities had anticipated this eventual flood of near boiling water and issued warnings for downstream residents. All but four — three badly burned and one drowned — watched the searing surge from the safety of high ground.

Once back in my home USGS office at Menlo Park, California, I was an instant in-demand lecturer to describe my El Chichon observations. Volcano talks were especially popular because the 1980 eruption of Mount St Helens was still fresh in the American public's mind. About the time I was tiring of my Mark-Twain-like lecture circuit, *serendipity* came calling.

Final lecture finished, as others were dispersing, a person in that audience approached me with the unexpected and startling news that I had just solved an intractable problem that was part of his brother-in-law's PhD thesis. Here's the short summary of our conversation.

In the 1960s, a PhD candidate in the anthropology program at Harvard University chose to collect and interpret tales of oral tradition carried by native inhabitants (Chamula Indians who are descendants of the Maya) of the part of Chiapas that includes El Chichon. One such tale was a puzzler for which he could never find a logical explanation. And that tale told of the destruction of a foregoing generation by a flood of boiling water. Floods were to be expected in this land of much rain, but a boiling flood? And so it happened that through subsequent contact from both me and his brother-in-law, Gary Gossen could now weave that last dangling bothersome thread of his PhD research into the orderly fabric of his thesis.

Follow-up geologic research at El Chichon has documented a history of several eruptions, similar to that of 1982, during at least the past two thousand years. The Mayans and their descendants of the region likely experienced several boiling floods of the Magdalena River. And what fantastic tales of oral history would such events provide!

Perhaps my most important take-away lesson from El Chichon is that broad communication, which is in fact the stuff of oral tradition, is a key ingredient to scientific progress. We scientists too often fail to look beyond the very artificial walls around our chosen specialties. Breaching such a barrier could serendipitously release a flood of opportunities and discoveries. But don't accept tales of yore simply on faith. Test. Test. Test!

PICKLES

SIXTY-THREE YEARS OLD and counting. I know that I'm just a youngster compared to my 95-year-old mother, but still, my tired legs are relieved when I find some shade beneath an overhanging ledge and scrunch down into a modified lotus position to enjoy a mid-day lunch that is tucked safely away in my backpack. Pele, my dog and faithful field companion, is also ready for a break from what has been a full morning of scrambling over hot and hilly terrain in search of something as mundane as rocks.

You see, I'm not the nerdy contemporary kind of geologist who spends hours staring into the bloodshot eye of a computer monitor, looking for electron-generated wisdom and inspiration. Nor am I the white-lab-coat variety, who mixes this chemical powder with that inert grunge, heats and squeezes the resulting brew, and believes that the nature of real rocks is illuminated by whatever the experiment produces. And I'm certainly not the type who develops grand mathematically supported theories of how the Earth should behave, and then has difficulty accepting the notion that what really happens in nature is not so neat, predicable, and shaped to fit into a calculated cubbyhole.

Yes, I use a computer, but only to write the occasional essay. I have never had the yen or talent to do lab work, and I can get bogged down with numbers when more than the four basic grade-school-level functions (addition, subtraction, multiplication, and division) are involved. Even these simple mathematical exercises of the mind have accumulated a patina of difficulty as I age. You see, I'm what's called an old field geologist. We hammer, examine through a magnifying lens, drop acid on, kick, and even lick rocks in their natural state to help push back the frontiers of earth science. Sometimes the frontiers push back pretty hard, but field geology is truly the bread and butter, or is it bread and pickles, of earth science.

Field geologists, young and old, tend to be rather ordinary folks who are prone to what some consider aberrant behavior. Those who study human personality types generally categorize us as rigidly ordered and introverted people, whose habits and preferred interactions with other humans border on the anti- if not a-social. I know, because I've been through the Myers-Briggs testing and evaluation required by my employer as part of career-enhancement training. You can imagine how far my self-esteem rose with the introduction of this bit of knowledge into my life. Ha! What do those behavioral scientists know, anyway!?

The fact is that a field geologist spends a lot of time alone, or only in the company of a non-human critter, like Pele. Field seasons spent walking over remote areas looking at rocks can account for a large part of a typical calendar year, and the rest of life in the office and at home may not include enough socializing to backfill the field-induced void. Some of us sure try to compensate, though.

As fallout from the hermit-like part of my life, I have had many lengthy and animated conversations with Pele, and her predecessors, and even with beef cattle, who have about as much gray matter as a slug. Feedback, of course, is minimal … maybe a canine bark and wagging tail, or perhaps a blank bovine stare followed by rapid retreat complete with the raised-tail diarrheic spray so typical of those beasts. This is a pretty disgusting reaction to my attempts at conversation. But as field geologists know, just the sound of one's own voice can be comforting and at least a partial substitute for real human company. And talking to almost any other living creature seems less silly and bizarre than talking to one's self.

If this strikes you as at all odd, consider the inflated importance of lunch-in-the-field to us rock beaters.

In the mind of a typically introverted and judgmental field geologist, the selection and preparation of a "correct" lunch is as sacred as communion is to a pastor or priest. After all, lunch is the fuel needed to keep the field body energized and productive, and I'm sure it feeds the soul, too. My colleagues and I have honed this food ritual to a piercingly religious art form that only its practitioners can properly appreciate. Probably as far back as the time of its invention by an earl of the same name, the *sandwich* has been the centerpiece of a proper lunch. And as those behavioral scientists would be quick to point out, day-to-day sandwich variety is fundamentally anathema to our personality type. A true field geologist would never want to be so adventuresome and flexible as to change his sandwich type. Well, maybe just once or possibly twice during a decades-long career, but any change would most certainly be for a profound personal reason.

On very special and rare occasions, geologists practice fieldwork in groups of two, or in even greater though usually single-digit numbers. From my observations at such uncomfortably crowded gatherings, I must conclude that peanut butter and jelly is the sandwich of choice.

Early in my career, I let myself be influenced, for a few days, by senior mentoring colleagues to the point that I actually tried this most popular food. What a mistake! A single bite quickly convinced me that there is only one effective way to get peanut butter off the roof of your mouth (with your index finger), just as there is only one effective way to get peanut butter off that finger (insert in mouth and scrape along the roof thereof, against the upper teeth). The energy spent in such an iterative eating process is about equivalent to the caloric value of the consumed food. But it sure is fun to feed it to a dog and watch the faces she makes.

Oral tradition within my profession speaks of bleached skeletons of geologists found in remote places, with index-finger bone in mouth and half-empty peanut butter jars nearby. I shun the risk of such demise. Besides, most of my fieldwork is in dry, hot, semi-arid and desert places, where viscid sticky peanut butter would make me even thirstier than I normally am. So, for self-defense and self-preservation, I have perfected the properly and adequately moist pickle-based sandwich, whose secrets I now share.

Take two pieces of bread (doesn't much matter what type, as you will soon understand) and thickly cover one side of each with a smooth layer of Miracle Whip Salad Dressing. Contrary to hosts of suggestions I've received over the years, mayonnaise will not do, nor will Hellman's attempt to imitate Miracle Whip. On one of these already tasty surfaces, add thin slices of a mild cheese in whatever pattern is needed to cover the dressing. Next comes the principal moisture-giving ingredient, a layer of bread-and-butter pickles, the kind that Mother made … literally, in my childhood home. These pickles come in slices about the size of a quarter, and typically, ten can be arranged to cover the cheese layer for conventionally shaped bread. However, *and here is the most important part of the sandwich-making process*, pickle slices straight from the jar to the sandwich provide so much moisture that by lunchtime the bread is a soggy, unappetizing, and nearly inedible saturated lump. So, each pickle slice must be sucked just enough to reduce its moisture content to an acceptable level. Not everyone can (or wants to) master this step, and most who succeed do so after several failures. Once the pickles are adequately sucked and properly positioned, slap the two slices of bread together, and insert the sandwich into a plastic baggie to preserve the proper moisture level for the noontime feast.

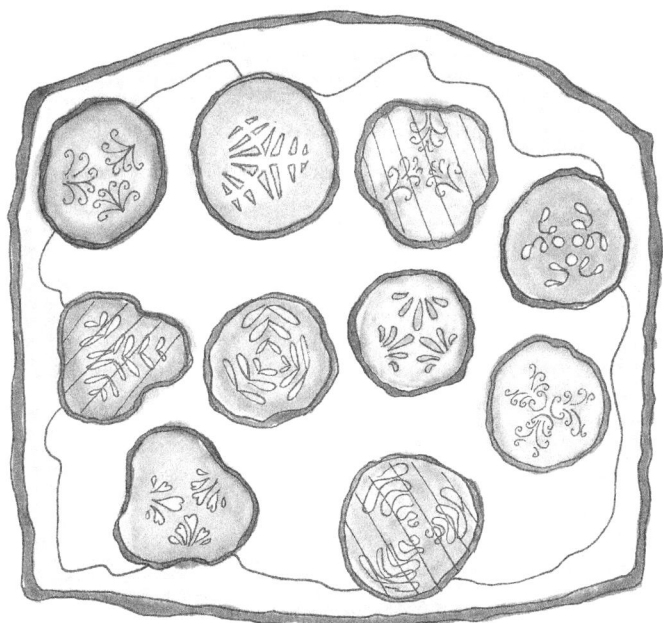

PICKLES ▪ 147

Enough mental meanderings. With Pele napping at my side, I carefully extract lunch from my backpack and bite into yet another pickle-ish culinary delight. Aaah. The texture, moisture content, and taste are optimum. Lunchtime perfection!! No peanut butter stickiness and enough sandwich moisture to help me comfortably ration out the drinking water I carry for the rest of the day.

As I'm enjoying this lunch in our shady rest spot, my mind inexplicably seizes on the realization that at a rate of about a hundred field days each year, I am eating the three-thousand-five-hundredth pickle sandwich of my geologic career. And I (am barely able to) mentally calculate that I have consumed nearly thirty-five-thousand pickle slices in the process. If one is what one eats, I should be a semi-sweet four-hundred-foot-tall greenish cylinder of swallowed slices accumulated as stacked-up discs. Thank goodness, this hasn't happened to me, yet, though my wife sometimes says that I'm semi sweet ... when I'm not repeating my hope that she will keep the house a bit more orderly. In recent years I *have* recognized a slightly shriveled dimpleness showing up in areas of formerly firm and svelte epidermis. Hmmmm. Cucumber skin or cellulite?

Lunch finished and my focus back on the reality of today's work, I roust Pele and we head off to look for more rocky outcrops to hammer, kick, and lick.

Sixty-three years old and counting. Still sucking pickles after all these years. I may be the most accomplished pickle sucker in my entire profession. And boy is it worth it, in spite of the occasional off-color joke that this habit elicits from some of my colleagues!

P.S. I sent a copy of this essay to Kraft Foods, the company that manufactures and markets Miracle Whip. Someone at Kraft sent me a coupon for a free jar of that tasty spread! It's not often I get paid for my essays.

A KILAUEA LESSON FOR LOVERS

Readers who are familiar with the staff and ongoing science at the Hawaiian Volcano Observatory during the period mentioned in the essay below should be able to assign real names to some characters. The mysterious email is a product of my imagination. But the geologic events described therein fairly accurately summarize what went on at HVO back in the day.

THE INBOX OF my personal email recently beeped the arrival of a rather intriguingly mysterious file whose title links the pulse of a well-known Hawaiian volcano with that of human lovers. With much trepidation I opened that file, fingers crossed that its access to desktop circuitry would not corrupt my HP Pavilion. The professional pull generated by having studied the titular volcano during the early years of my career in geology was stronger than my resistance to possibly triggering yet another digital crash-and-burn caused by self-centered curiosity.

Having now read and pondered the mysterious message about Kilauea, in hindsight I know I made the correct decision with the left click of my mouse. The file verifies a behavioral link that I have long felt between my first volcano and my conjugal life.

I wish to share the story with other lovers of volcanoes and lovers of, well, love. The use of pronouns replicates the tale as sent to me. No names were attached. The message apparently represents the recently typed hand-written notes of a geologist who was part of a team that studied Kilauea long before small portable computers served science. The story describes early years of research at the Hawaiian Volcano Observatory, popularly known as HVO. It reads like a personal diary. The action described began in 1958, while I was still in high school.

November 15, 1959: It's 4AM, and I'm about to grab a couple hours rest from our frantic scramble to keep tabs on a mega eruption that began last night. But before sawing some wood, I'll jot down a few notes about this big event. It all began last year.

A master key to getting a firm grip on what was happening underground, down in the bowels of Kilauea between eruptions, was turned during the autumn of 1958 shortly after the staff here at HVO finished installing an array of seismometers across the summit area of the volcano. From then on we've been able to record the seismic shakings and tremblings of the mountain and use those data to map the hypocenters of quakes that originate within the heart of Kilauea. No more guessing about the where and what of these temblors' origins!

Suddenly, we were able to reasonably surmise a long history of periodic violence that we had suspected from interpretation of the badly broken surface lavas of Kilauea. Over time, the internally generated grumbling and rumbling of earthquakes has literally busted up the volcano. We had no big surprise there.

But here's what showed up as a kicker surprise with our newly installed recorders at Kilauea. One unique type of ground shaking produced an entirely unexpected shape of tracing on the Observatory seismograms.

We were initially dubious about the meaning of the pattern. Maybe there was something afoul with the electronics of our machines? That was said to be very unlikely, by our electronics technician. Multitudinous bursts of the bizarre pattern were recorded repeatedly over a period of days to months, from 1958 to the day I write these words in 1959. Eventually, we cautious scientists bravely (ha!) concluded that we were seeing a truly new expression of Kilauea's inter-eruption unrest.

The new seismic tracings came with no human-felt shaking of the ground. They apparently were the result of a far too weak and subtle force for that. Yet they were mind bending ... and boring. Mind bending, because they were unique in seismic history. (And all of us research scientists know that we live to discover new things about nature!) Boring, because they went on and on and on, with absolutely no variation in the shape or frequency of their paper-chart trace. We were dealing with one-cycle-per-second monotony. One staff joker described this unitary hertz as a foreign thorn in our collective side, Hertz being a German scientist for whom such repetitious cycles are named.

Our hertz was a constant-amplitude wave form ... up and down and up and down etc ... somewhat like a pond-surface wave generated when a rock is thrown in. But those pond waves quickly die out. So does the wavy pattern generated on seismic charts by the ground shaking during a conventional earthquake.

Several staff meetings aimed at developing a scientific explanation for our discovery ended in frustration. All we could agree on was to call the new thing Harmonic Tremor. But then just yesterday the amateur church organist (our geochemist) interrupted his customary low humming of hymnals with a "Eureka! I've got it!!" shout.

"Team," he said, "I think that we're recording the pulsing flow of magma rising through Kilauea on its way to eruption. It's playing a tune for us, just like air does when it surges through a pipe of my church's organ. I think that unusual magma-generated signal may be able to tell us where and when the next eruption will happen. All we have to do is chart the depth where the pulsing originates and map the bulls-eye spot at Kilauea's surface that the rising pulse is aimed at! We've got a monotone guiding us on its way to giving life to a new layer of surface lava!"

During his Eureka moment, I scribbled notes.

Then, with a shared feeling of a possible major scientific accomplishment, we dispersed late that afternoon (Hey that's just yesterday. It seems a lot longer ago.) and headed home to our families while the tremor of good old Johnny one-note continued to saturate our seismometers.

My wife had prepared a tasty mahi mahi dish for dinner, which *we savored as I explained the professional excitement of the day. She nodded her approval of my enthusiasm as I talked about earthquakes and the newly named harmonic tremor that was shaking our seismic instruments at one wave-cycle per second. "That's one hertz in professional talk. Named for ... you probably already guessed it ... a German scientist named Hertz. That's spelled h e r t z" I added, knowing that she would mentally file the pronunciation and spelling of that word in her growing vocabulary learned from a husband wedded to his career nearly as much as to her.*

Later that night, perhaps in part a result of more-than-adequate white wine with the mahi mahi, we made gentle love that generated a steadily sloshing rhythm in the liquid bladder of our waterbed. As we finished and lay supine in parallel exhaustion, she whispered, "Aaaah. I love that love ... that hertz."

I glowed in the satisfaction of knowing that her closing word was not its painful homophone. We dozed off mutually content.

Shortly thereafter, a phone call informed me that Kilauea had begun to erupt ... at about the time that my love and I had slipped between the sheets. The volcano's harmonic tremor that our team had named, interpreted, and seen recording during yesterday afternoon's discussion had indeed represented the rise of molten rock. And that hot sticky fluid is now spurting into a deep pit crater called Kilauea Iki.

I feel a closer-than-ever bond with both wife and the current object of my career. Life is good! Fantastic!!

Well readers, there you have it. An unusual tale that links love of science to love of human life. Whoever the anonymous sender of the email is, I heartily thank you. You rekindled memories that I shall never forget, of my 1970s days on the staff at the Hawaiian Volcano Observatory. Perhaps your diary contains other intriguing messages? You know my email address.

KACHINA JUSTICE

I was inspired to write this piece by Grant Allen's "The Thames Valley Catastrophe" in Science Fiction by the Rivals of H.G. Wells (edited by Alan Kingsley, 1979). Allen describes a lava flow that snaked its way down the valley of the Thames until it entered, and partly destroyed, London. My tale about Flagpole is somewhat more believable. In fact, replace Flagpole with Flagstaff, Arizona, and much of the story is true.

HINDSIGHT IS A convenient crutch if one wishes to sound intelligent while trying to convince others that a failure was not a failure. So this crutch served me well each time I proclaimed "I could have told you so, if you had but ..." during the post-mortem period of what came to be known as *Kachina Justice* in our little mountain town some miles south of a deep canyon of much grandeur.

My mistake, only recognized in hindsight, was to have repeatedly — during a decade-long span of public lectures and coffee-sipping gab sessions — made bold pronouncements of what Mother Nature held in store for the future of my recently adopted community. Being highly educated in the ways of volcanoes, careless wanderings outside the bounds of the scientific method, perhaps compounded by a bit of hubris, lured me to also pontificate on floods, earthquakes, and even forest conflagrations, while actually knowing nothing out of the ordinary about these other topics.

In so doing, I unwittingly developed the reputation of a community expert in the ways of nature, while in fact I was a mediocre naturalist at best. So in spite of my publicly perceived superior knowledge, I may have been even blinder than many of my Flagpole fellow citizens concerning what was fermenting within our lofty Sainted Mountain at the edge of town during the years 2017 and 2018. In hindsight is seems that even my volcano training was lacking.

A day of unforeseen disaster fell on the Ides of March, 2018. *"Five hundred recreationists killed at Snowbowel. Some drowned and others burned to a crisp by lava!!"* proclaimed the following day's headline of the *Flagpole Moonshine*, in its predictably unsubtle explanation of community happenings. *"Downstream flooding kills hundreds more in Badgerville and the greater Flagpole community. Three hundred homes destroyed!"* cried out the subtitle for an exposé that occupied the entire twenty-four page edition.

It truly was a horrific event that overwhelmed Flagpolians and out-of-town snow bunnies on March 15 of that year. There was no escape for those in nature's crosshairs when the town's ancient and revered volcano, upon whose snowy slopes people frolicked, shot back to life on a bucolic spring afternoon.

On that news-making Thursday, my sturdy hindsight crutch told me that, from my beginnings as a recent transplant to Flagpole, I should not have casually dismissed tales spun by village Elders. These members of second- and third-generation families understood that their town was surrounded by hundreds of volcanoes, the youngest of which had buried nearby Sinagua Village with a thick blanket of cinders less than a thousand years earlier. Their premonition that something like this might happen again, soon, proved to be prescient.

I often met with such senior citizens over a cup of coffee at the Peak View Cafe. Weather permitting, we occupied sidewalk tables, which offered an unobstructed view of the state's loftiest elevation … the Sainted Mountain. Knowing of my advanced training in volcanoes, one or another of the Elders would direct our conversation to Vulcan's domain, after the recent social town gossip was dispensed with. Volcano-speak usually began with a review of the demise of the unfortunate Sinagua Village. Many of the Elders looked old enough to have witnessed that millennium-old event. Then, the following kind of coffee-klatch session invariably followed.

"Never mind about the Sinagua disaster," I began, feeling comfortable in my cloak of higher education. "That's ancient history. Fear not that another eruption will harm our lovely forested Limestone Plateau. Even if it soon should, extremely unlikely though that may be, science tells us that any eruption would strike far to the east, sparing our lovely town."

Though too polite to audibly dispute my views on the behavior of volcanoes, facial expressions projected silent doubt of my advice. Their lingering unease encouraged me to continue.

"Yet, if you are of a personality that must fear some natural disaster" — I pretended to ignite a stick match drawn along my zippered levis fly, light a cigarette and then toss the still-flaming match over my shoulder — "never ever play with fire." I punctuated this admonition with a gesture toward nearby dry ponderous pines of our local landscape. At this point, Elder Burns extinguished the pleasant smelling mixture of tobacco smoldering in his Briar Pipe.

Then a self-anointed spokesman for the Elders decided to challenge my assurances that volcanoes were not our community's imminent enemy. He gazed northward at the Sainted Mountain, the towering centerpiece of our hilly homeland, and extended an arthritic index finger generally toward the thirteen-thousand-foot top, a prominence so tall that it remained snow-covered through the summer.

"Look, young man," he commanded, finger bobbing at the peak. "Look to that patch of snow-free outcropping high on the mountain."

I respectfully obeyed, as any properly reared person of a younger generation would when addressed by his Elder.

"For as long as I've lived here, and my father and his father before him, that one place has never been covered with snow. Not even during the wintriest of years." His fellow sages nodded, murmuring their assent.

"That spot is hot," he added, staring searingly at me, in hopes of burning a niche into the wall of my contrary view. "The mountain may be as wrinkled and weary-looking as we Elders. But it is *alive!*"

His eyes flashed an animated gleam, perhaps in recollection of scaling the peak as an athletic youth. "One day you'll see. Yes, one day you'll understand."

A somewhat awkward stern-faced silence followed ... a mute though unmistakable expression of agreement within the Elder group.

Respectful, though not willing to concede their view unchallenged, I softly replied "I think not. Many trained scientists before me have visited that spot of which you speak. They report that it is a cliff of ancient black volcanic rock bearing the name *basalt*."

Mention of basalt triggered a cacophony of Elder recollections about how basalt had been the culprit at Sinagua Village. I continued when the babble subsided.

"That outcropping is so precipitous that only the most tenacious of mountain lichen can thrive thereon. Snow, as men as wise as you would surely agree, does not ... it simply cannot attach itself to a cliff. Besides, the cliff faces south, toward the sun. Even if snow could conveniently suspend the law of gravity at that place ... a fairy tale of the highest order ... the sun's warming rays would quickly melt the frozen stuff."

There were no arguments against the reality of gravity and the warming strength of the sun's rays. And so our gathering ended in friendly agreement to disagree on some issues, and to meet again soon for further discussion. Elders departed, certain of their wisdom accumulated through time and life's experiences. I strolled toward my Mountain Campus office, feeling positive of my superior knowledge and understanding of nature, attested to by a framed and proudly displayed parchment diploma from The Farm, a California university of some repute.

Our coffee conferences went on like this for a decade, with no definitive progress toward agreeing to the level of threat of a new eruption and the reason for the snow-free disposition of the south-facing outcropping high on the slopes of the Sainted Mountain.

Then the changes began. The material excesses of *Homo sapiens* around the globe increasingly polluted Earth's atmosphere with invisible life-threatening carbonaceous gases. The Keeling Curve of Mauna Loa suddenly became as well known as that of any successful major-league baseball pitcher. Soon, an entirely new hyphenated word was introduced into the English language to describe the phenomenon.

People began to speak about the *carbon-footprints* of nations and of individuals, as though these were irremovable stains on the carpet of Earth's biosphere. Many hands of all cultures were wrung in the anxiety of what these filthy tracks portended for the future of humankind. Governments made promises ... some even passed laws ... to reduce the size of their footprints, though no progress was made as human populations continued to grow and consume, grow and consume. In ultimate cynical foolishness, footprint allotments were bought and sold on volatile capitalist markets, purportedly in the belief that changing ownership of a lethal substance can somehow defuse it.

All attempts at solutions failed. The dreaded carbon-footprints continued to grow toward a size that no shoe or life-supporting environment could long abide.

Flagpole and the Sainted Mountain were not spared the effects of global warming that came with poisoned air. For the first time in Elder memories, winter's mountain-top blanket of snow disappeared completely around midsummer. They, of course, saw this change as proof that the Mountain was not only hot, but was developing a stronger volcanic fever with each passing year.

"Bosh!" I countered. "Earth's warming climate is the source of extra heat. Even the world's glaciers are melting. And soon you residents of Flagpole will want air conditioners installed in your homes."

Another change occurred on the Sainted Mountain following the first summer of no snowy cover. Adding yet one more to a long history of snubs to Native American cultural values, the nation's Supremes awarded Snowbowel the right to cover the winter-season slopes of the Sainted Mountain with artificial snow made from the treated sewage of Flagpole. Thus the owners of that snow-play area were able to extend the ski season from three to five months. The powerful rumbling of snow-making equipment shook the mountain for hours on end in this successful endeavor to bring longer snow-play seasons and expanded profits to the Snowbowel enterprise.

My friends the town Elders felt certain that the new shaking was that of an increasingly unstable Sainted Mountain, the volcano becoming more and more restless as its temperature rose. "Double bosh!!" I replied. "Go stand beneath one of the snow-making behemoths if you doubt that they are the source of ground tremors."

Each side of our debating society persisted so in its view, until Mother Nature interrupted our Peak View Cafe gathering of March 15, 2018. What we witnessed that day was cataclysmic. Like a pulled zipper releasing the insulated warmth beneath a parka, a gaping fissure opened within a minute from the steep black outcropping of snow-free basalt to the bottom of the Snowbowel chair lift, allowing fiery red lava to ooze from the crack. Flowing molten rock instantly melted natural and man-made snow in its downhill path. We watched as the snout of this monstrous gathering of water and lava, shrouded in steam, cascaded downward for the few seconds it took to disappear from our view on its path toward Badgerville. Knowing the downstream path from there, we fled to safety atop Bison Park and watched as the low-lying floodplains of Flagpole were inundated with boiling hot water. The lava itself would soon follow.

I snapped awake. *What a scary dream!* I stared up into cloying darkness ... soaking in sweat, not sure of the place. I floundered in the disorientation that often comes with waking in an unfamiliar room.

I snaked my hand beneath the bedcovers until it encountered the familiar warmth of a woman's curved hip. I moved the hand up, between our pillows, and there found the sleeping ball of fur named Marza, the family cat. I was at home.

I raised my head and looked beyond the foot of the bed to a shelf that held the emerald-green time-keeping eye of our Bose radio. I squinted to improve the focus of aging vision and saw 4:00 AM. The sounds of NPR's "Morning Edition" would begin automatically in two more hours.

Aaaah. Now relieved and relaxed, I remembered that I was scheduled to lecture about our local volcanoes to a group of senior citizens later in the day. My mind flashed to the disturbing dream, not yet vanished into the ether of forgotten sleep-time mental meanderings.

Egads! Today is March 15. A bad day for Julius Caesar, but not for me or Flagstaff ... I hope. Still, I'm gonna be more upfront, a lot less dogmatic than usual when I talk about the possibility of a future eruption hitting our town. There's Sunset. And now even SP, Strawberry, and O'Neill Craters may have erupted when people were around. What's next? I'm not a superstitious guy, but that dream I just woke from … zounds!

I laid back and drifted into sleep, with Marza purring in my left ear and with me hoping to be awakened later by a familiar, reassuring, and mellifluous female KNAU voice, which might start my Ides day with some upbeat news.

THE VOLCANO THAT WASN'T
A Tale for Practitioners of Geologic Field Mapping ... and Other Thinking People

IN THE MID 1990s I was asked to lead a team of U.S. Geological Survey (USGS) geologists to map a large volcano (named Alid) and its immediate surroundings in Eritrea. The ultimate goal of this project was to evaluate Alid and its potentially hot magmatic roots for geothermal resources that might be tapped to generate electricity.

Eritrea was then a newly created country, just recently split off from Ethiopia. In map view the country has the shape of a tilted funnel whose tail points southeastward toward Djibouti. Eritrea's north-facing boundary is along the south coast of the Red Sea. Inland to the southwest, into the bowl of the funnel, the land surface steps abruptly upward across a series of geologic fault escarpments, to nearly eight thousand feet elevation where a plateau houses the capital city Asmara and surrounding farm land. This new vibrant Eritrea was in the process of assessing natural resources that the nation might tap in support of its people.

The U.S. Government offered help, including our geothermal project. Hot springs and steam vents were already known on Alid, and this two-thousand-foot-tall mountain is surrounded by geologically young basalt lava flows that were erupted within a NW/SE trending lowland (called the Danakil Depression) that is a barely-above-sea-level part of a system of widening fissures that periodically erupt. This geologic context is a favorable environment within which to locate targets for drilling into reservoirs of hot high-pressure aquifers and associated steam. Towering Alid was a logical target to start with.

So USGS colleagues Mike Clynne, Jake Lowenstern, and Jim Smith joined me in planning a field season for mapping and sampling the rocks, hot water, and steam that Alid had to offer. We would camp near the foot of Alid, on an arid and very sparsely populated plain where a well serves as the only source of fresh water to local nomads and their camels and goats. In our preparations, we searched the geologic literature for published information about Alid. We found one seemingly useful publication. Several years earlier, French and Italian geologists had reconnoitered Alid and its surroundings. A paragraph of their report shaped our general expectations of what we would find there.

"Alid is located at the northern apex of the Danakil Depression, between the Salt Plain to the south and the Gulf of Zula to the north. Three units are easily distinguished there: the central silicic complex (stratovolcano and ignimbrites), the northern, and the southern lava fields. ***The silicic complex is a typical stratovolcano mainly made of pyroclastic products with scarce silicic lava flows and crowned by a caldera.****"* {Emphasis added}

The French geologist who coauthored this report is a personal friend. I contacted him, and he assured me that our USGS team would have a productive time discovering the details of that towering caldera-topped stratovolcano.

Mike, Jake, Jim, and I flew to Asmara where we met Eritrean geologists who would work with us. Together we purchased camp supplies and headed toward Alid in their jeeps. Road access within the Danakil Depression is bare-track primitive, mostly over the rough original surface of basalt lava flows.

We established camp on day one and began field work on day

two. By day four, our traverses up and across Alid indicated that what we had expected to map as a stratovolcano was not a volcano of any sort. The short version of our discoveries, after many days of scrambling over and mapping Alid, is that the mountain is a structural dome. Apparently, a shallow body of highly viscous magma accumulated beneath that location in the Danakil Depression, and as the volume of magma increased it pushed upward enough to bend overlying preexisting rocks into a steep-sided domal mountain — a shape that from a distance is stratovolcano-like in appearance. But as some wise philosopher is rumored to have posited, looks can be deceiving.

The girdling flanks of the dome are mostly tilted-up basalt lava flows. These are the older forerunners to the younger horizontal basalt lava flows that surround Alid — the north and south lava fields of the French/Italian report. The so-called caldera, at the top of Alid, is mostly a product of ongoing erosion that has already removed enough from the dome's top to expose Precambrian rocks, which are the ancient geologic underpinnings for all of the young volcanic rocks of this region.

Perhaps the most significant geothermal-energy indicator is that some of the viscous magma eventually erupted at the top of Alid in the form of rhyolite pumice and lava (the ignimbrites and silicic lava flows of the French/Italian team). Geothermal steam suitable for spinning the turbines of an electrical power plant is commonly created around bodies of rhyolitic magma.

Now nearly twenty years after my time at Alid, when I think back on that project I'm reminded of lessons learned incrementally during my half-century career as a field geologist. One lesson cautions against creating a geologic map without actually first walking the terrain. That story is described on earlier pages of this book ("Remembering Siemon "Si" Muller"). Apparently, the French/Italian team spent little, if any, time actually climbing the slopes of Alid.

Along my career path I also absorbed another bit of valuable advice (for all thinkers, not just geologists) from reading "The Periodic Table," by Primo Levi. He writes, "There is trouble in store for anyone who surrenders to the temptation of mistaking an elegant hypothesis for certainty." The words of the French/Italian report state without doubt that Alid is a stratovolcano. A few words of uncertainty would have been appropriate.

Some of my professional colleagues know that I loathe seeing the words *clear* and *clearly* in geological literature. Silly though this may sound, I'm of the ilk who subscribe to the notion that the only certain (clear) thing in *Homo sapiens* life is some ever-present level of uncertainty. We scientists work to reduce that to a useful level.

I sent my French colleague a copy of our Alid report, shortly after it appeared in the late 1990s. Mon ami and I have continued to communicate via snail and email right up to 2015. Neither of us has chosen to raise the topic of that enigmatic Alid.

A GRAND TIME AT GRAND FALLS

TWENTY THOUSAND YEARS ago, a volcano about thirty-five miles east of Flagstaff, Arizona, erupted very fluid basalt lava. The runny stuff flowed several miles further east down a gentle slope, where it spilled into the deep narrow canyon of what would later be named the Little Colorado River. Lava filled the canyon and spilled over onto the far side for a few hundred yards. Eventually, water filled the newly created upstream reservoir, then found its way around the edge of the far-side lava spill-over and cascaded into the downstream part of the canyon on its trip to join the Colorado River, of Grand Canyon fame. Today, that cascade is called Grand Falls. The vertical drop equals that of honeymooners' favorite Niagara Falls, although Grand Falls flows only ephemerally during spring snow melt and summer monsoon rain downpours.

Grand Falls during spring runoff. Black lava of the volcanic dam is barely visible on the right. The horizontal layers of the falls are ancient sedimentary-rock formations.

In May of 2003, I led a field trip to Grand Falls for sixth grade students of DeMiguel School of Flagstaff. At the end of my show-and-tell, teacher Rosemary Hume asked each student to write a short essay about what he/she learned on the trip. I joined the students with the following.

MY STORY OF GRAND FALLS

First came the canyon, real deep not so wide.
Water ran through it, with plants on the side.

Then came the lava, quite runny and hot.
It spilled in the canyon and filled up the spot.

Next came erosion that washed rocks away,
To carve the new canyon that we see today.

Finally came students to study this stuff,
With help from their teacher
And a geologist named Duff.

AN UNFORGETTABLE MEET-THE-PRESS MOMENT ON THE ALASKAN PENINSULA

IN 1977 A volcanic eruption occurred on the Alaskan Peninsula, near the south shore of Becharof Lake, where no volcano previously existed. There were famous youthful volcanic neighbors, including the legendary Valley of Ten Thousand Smokes several miles to the north and lovely Aniakchak Caldera about that distance to the south. But this time a blade of basalt magma knifed its way up through some deposits of mixed boulders and sand left by a somewhat earlier glacier, and blasted out two new craters through a patch of volcano-free ground. The place has been named Ukinrek.

The principal active crater at Ukinrek during the eruption of 1977. Photo courtesy of Alaska Department of Fish and Game.

One crater is rather small in diameter and depth and has been pretty much ho-hum ignored by geologists and tourists alike. But bigger brother/sister is a quasi-circular hole a quarter-mile-wide and few hundred feet deep, partly filled with water. The surrounding landscape is mantled with the 1977 vintage basaltic cinders plus some intermixed pieces of the glacial debris through which the magma wedged and then exploded its way to the surface. There's much more to the geologic story of the eruption, but that's not to the purpose of this essay.

The main Ukinrek Crater as of 1993. The light-colored rocks just above lake level are the glacial deposits through which the eruption occurred. The layered dark deposits above the glacial host and in the surrounding black blanket are the products of the 1977 eruption. Photo courtesy of David Lescinsky.

I was a member of a three-person team that visited Ukinrek in 1993 to sample the 1977 deposits, top to bottom, in the walls of the crater and in a series of holes that we dug within the surrounding cinder blanket. Geologists Michael Ort, Vicki McConnell, and I comprised that team.

Somehow the NBC TV affiliate in Anchorage learned of our project and dispatched a reporter and her camera man to interview us and document our project. Lacking road access, they, like the three of us, arrived via a single-engine pontoon plane. They set up a tent near our encampment and spent two days interviewing us and photographing our field activities.

One particular interview question, and all this time later I can't remember the specific question, elicited this honest answer. "Geologists don't know." That reply became a central part of the reporter's product, completed mostly at our camp site. We three watched during the filming, and were barely able to stifle laughter as we listened to said reporter repeatedly stumble over the pronunciation of the word *geologists*. It kept coming out as *geogolists*, although eventually, after many retakes, she got it right. It took about the same number of retakes for this reporter to satisfactorily manage her makeup and hair-styling in the typical Alaskan Peninsula wind.

Back home, a few days after I told this tale to my wife Anne, she surprised me with a new sweatshirt emblazoned in bold white print with GEOGOLISTS DON'T KNOW. It's been a great conversation piece at parties. I still have that cherished gift, although over many years of laundering it has shrunk (or has my girth increased?) from my size to Anne's.

Anne models my favorite sweatshirt.

Now fast forward to the year 2013: Anne and I have recently moved from Flagstaff, Arizona, to Greenbank, Washington, a village on Whidbey Island in Puget Sound. We are walking our Doberman at the Greenbank Farm, which offers a wonderful network of paths where dogs-off-leash are invited. We meet another dog walker, and in the custom of this park-like place we stop to chat with her about dog things — breed characteristics and such. Dog owners will understand the drift of the conversation.

Suddenly, in mid sentence this person pauses, looks straight at me, and loudly blurts, "I know you. You're Wendell Duffield, and you study volcanoes. We met in Alaska. Remember?!" Anne and I were both taken aback (perhaps for somewhat different reasons? ☺).

No, I didn't remember, in the sense that I did not recognize this particular person. But a bit of Ukinrek reminiscing proved that she was the geogolist-spouting NBC TV reporter from Anchorage, and like me, she is a dog lover who now lives near Greenbank Farm. And that my readers, is a simple tale of *it's a small world, after all.*

She said she has no memory of her problem pronouncing the word geologist. Her final reportage piece aired nationally with perfect word pronunciation. (Do people selectively tend to wipe out weaknesses/mistakes from their long-term memory bank?)

I explained that her geogolist flubs were one of, if not the most poignant and entertaining of my memories from the Ukinrek experience. (Do people selectively tend to remember other people's foibles, rather than their own?)

Hoot! Hoot! My career in volcanology has been super interesting in so many human, as well as scientific ways! I wonder what tomorrow will bring. This geogolist doesn't know.

This just in...
Geogolists Don't Know!

AN UNFORGETTABLE MEET-THE-PRESS MOMENT • 171

ARE THE HEADWATERS OF THE MISSISSIPPI RIVER IN SOUTH DAKOTA?

A **LOUD** *NO* answer to the question posed by the title of this essay likely seems obvious to anyone who has been exposed to even just a smattering of education in current geography. Check any reputable published map of rivers in Minnesota and you will see that the Mississippi originates at Lake Itasca, in the northern part of that state. From there, a small stream meanders first northward, and then eastward and finally southward, growing in size along the way, until it joins one of the state's other large rivers, the Minnesota, in the twin cities of Minneapolis and St. Paul.

Until I became a professional geologist, via a BA from Carleton College followed by MS and PhD degrees from Stanford University, I never thought to question the validity of the Itasca origins for the Mississippi. Shucks, as a six-year-old kid I even successfully jumped from stone to stone, placed across the stream outlet from Itasca at the site called the source of the Mississippi. I, similar to thousands of nimble-footed people before and after me, could therefore congratulate myself for walking across the mighty Mississippi without getting my feet wet! But now, nearly seven decades later, I know enough of the geologic story behind the development of Upper Midwest river systems to suggest that the Little Minnesota River originating near the South Dakota town of Veblen is a candidate for the headwaters of the Mississippi. Look out, Itasca!

I'm a son of South Dakota, born in Sisseton, which is not far from Veblen. Okay. I'm not truly a South Dakotan. My home town is

Browns Valley, Minnesota, barely across the state boundary, ten miles east of Sisseton. Browns Valley had neither doctor nor hospital in May of 1941. And Mother was not interested in home birthing. So Dad drove her up and out of town to the nearest suitable medical facility. The valley in which that town is nestled is a key feature supporting my contention that South Dakota can lay claim to the source of the Mississippi. Here's how the story goes.

Circa 14,000 to Circa 12,000 Years Ago

The most recent North American continental glacier covered almost all of Canada (maybe a few mountain peaks poked through out west) and most of the northern tier of our USA states. This huge mass of ice began to melt and retreat slowly northward around 14,000 years ago. With continuing melt and retreat, a certain gigantic lake formed in front of the glacier. At its maximum size, this lake (named Agassiz for a famous nineteenth-century Swiss glaciologist who carried out much of his research in the United States) covered much of northwestern Minnesota, eastern North Dakota, a bit of northeastern South Dakota, and a whole lot of Canada.

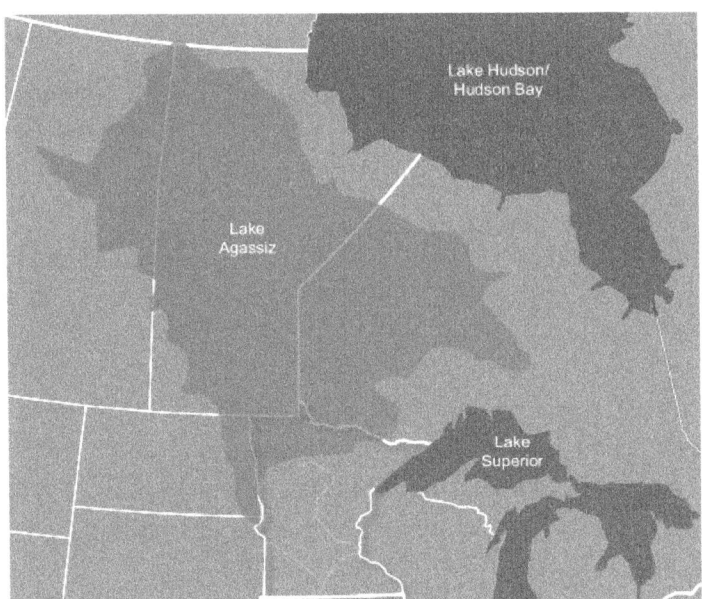

The approximate maximum extent of glacial Lake Agassiz.

Along its southerly facing margins, Lake Agassiz's water was contained primarily by long ridges of rock debris (called glacial moraines) that had been pushed and carried into place by the glacier. To the north, the retreating front of the glacier itself completed the shore line encompassing the lake.

With more and more ice melting and a concomitant rise in lake level, the rocky moraine deposits on the south were overtopped. About twelve thousand years ago, water began to flow through a breach outlet at the south tip of the lake and quickly eroded a broad deep channel across the landscape. This river (the forerunner of today's Minnesota River) would much later be named glacial River Warren for a mid-nineteenth-century land surveyor of the region. Small tributaries began to feed in from both sides. One would much later be named the Little Minnesota River and flow smack dab through my hometown.

The outflow through glacial River Warren was of gigantic epic proportions. At its maximum, the volume of water per unit time (often reported for rivers as cubic feet per second, cfs) was far greater than that pouring into the Gulf of Mexico at the mouth of today's Mississippi River. This massive flow eroded out an impressive valley — locally as much as four hundred feet deep and four miles wide — the pathway for today's Minnesota River. Further downstream, glacial River Warren's water was largely responsible for creating the valley that contains today's Mississippi River southward from the Twin Cities area.

While glacial River Warren was sculpting this landscape, a much smaller tributary was feeding in from the north at what would much later become the site of the Twin Cities. This tributary today is recognized as the farthest upstream reach of the Mississippi. However, the volume of flow and the erosive power of glacial River Warren were so much greater than those of this tributary that downward erosion of the bed of the tributary could not keep pace with that of Warren. I'll explain more about the possible significance of this disparity later.

Circa 12,000 to Circa 9,500 Years Ago

The melting front of the glacier eventually retreated far enough to open outflow channels eastward and northward from Lake Agassiz, with connections to the north Atlantic and Arctic Oceans. For some uncertain period of time, water simultaneously escaped at the east, north, and south outlets of Agassiz. With continuing outflow, about nine thousand five hundred years ago the lake surface dropped and stayed at a level below the elevation at the head of glacial River Warren, the future site of Browns Valley. After that, Warren was fed simply by rainfall and snowmelt, including input from downstream tributaries.

Two shallow finger-like lakes, which would much later be named Traverse and Big Stone, occupied part of Warren's valley near its now-dry connection to Agassiz. Many Native Americans must have watched in awe through this evolution from gigantic river to a couple of small lakes. Imagine the colorful and perhaps mystical tales of mind-challenging oral history passed from generation to generation!

One of these early inhabitants of the region was ceremoniously buried with some of his possessions in a gravel bar of River Warren. It's uncertain what the depth of flow, if any, was at that time; the top of the gravel bar is below the nearby rim elevation of Warren's channel. The surface of Lake Agassiz must have been significantly below its maximum elevation by burial time.

The burial site is within my hometown. The human remains, called the Browns Valley Man, were discovered in 1933 by William Jensen, a local amateur archaeologist. Carbon-fourteen dating of the human bones suggests that the Browns Valley Man is one of the oldest documented human inhabitants known for North America.

Several earlier generations of Native Americans certainly viewed the river when it was at full strength, many times the size of the present-day downstream Mississippi counterpart. Relatives and other friends on opposite river banks would have had a difficult time getting together for social occasions. There would have been no wading across, even with a gravel bar in mid channel!

Circa 9,500 Years Ago to the Twenty-First Century

Perhaps not much less than nine thousand years ago, the glacier had melted northward and Agassiz had drained enough to expose the system of lakes and rivers across the Upper Midwest and adjacent Canada in essentially the pattern of surface waters that decorate the landscape today. Glacial River Warren was no longer tapping into Lake Agassiz water. The area that would become Minnesota had its ten thousand lakes. Lake Traverse and Big Stone Lake were long shallow ponds, remnants of a once mighty through-flowing glacial River Warren.

As one result of land reconfiguration caused by glacial scouring, the site of Browns Valley emerged as a north/south drainage divide. The Little Minnesota River flows in there from the west (South Dakota) on its path to Big Stone Lake. It has deposited a low delta on which, together with the burial gravel bar, most of the town is built. The river commonly floods the low parts of the town during spring snowmelt.

At drier times of the year, from some spot near the house where I grew up, half of a theoretical raindrop flows northward while the other half heads south. Via Traverse and the Red River, the north half will arrive at Lake Winnipeg, the largest remnant of Agassiz, and continue on to Hudson Bay. Via Big Stone Lake, the other half will get to the Gulf of Mexico by way of the Minnesota and Mississippi Rivers.

But wait! Could the trip of that semi-droplet be via the *true* Mississippi River all the way southward? Some evidence contained in the landscapes of the region argues for a yes answer.

Veblen Versus Lake Itasca

Consider the amount of water that the Minnesota and Mississippi Rivers bring to their confluence at the Twin Cities. The amount varies with seasonal and geographic differences for each of the two watersheds. Averaged over years, the discharge of the Mississippi is somewhat larger. I view this difference as analogous to the relative sizes of a couple of sibling children, rather than that between a parent and child.

As my Grandpa Weeks used to say about comparisons, "Look carefully at the facts and think about what you see; then you shouldn't mistake a branch for the trunk of a tree." If he were still with us, I'm pretty sure Grandpa would decide that there is no substantive bigger-is-better argument to justify using the name Mississippi for the river path from Itasca to the Twin Cities. He'd more likely suggest that the Itasca and Minnesota Rivers are quasi-equal tributaries joining forces at the Twin Cities to create the Mississippi. I vote for that idea. With their greater age and experience, Grandpas are commonly wiser than the younger generations!

Now compare the size of the river valleys upstream of their confluence. As mentioned earlier, parts of the Minnesota are up to four miles wide and four hundred feet deep. Thank you glacial River Warren! Meanwhile, the valley of the Mississippi between Itasca and the Twin Cities is like a surficial scratch on an otherwise nearly planar surface.

Next ponder the fact that the Mississippi River within Minneapolis includes the two-hundred-foot-high Saint Anthony waterfall (modified in the mid twentieth century by concrete retaining walls plus locks to permit through-going boat traffic). The falls originated, near the present location of Fort Snelling, where the Minnesota and Mississippi Rivers join, in part because the pace of erosional lowering of the river bed by water coming down from Itasca was far less than that of the bed of River Warren. Once Warren lost water input from Lake Agassiz and the river level dropped, the bed of the Mississippi at the confluence was left hanging as a waterfall. Grandpa's thoughts about branches and trunks may fit this situation. During the time since that waterfall first became exposed (around nine thousand years ago), it has migrated upstream stepwise, by erosional undercutting at the base that triggers repeated collapse at the top, to its current location in Minneapolis.

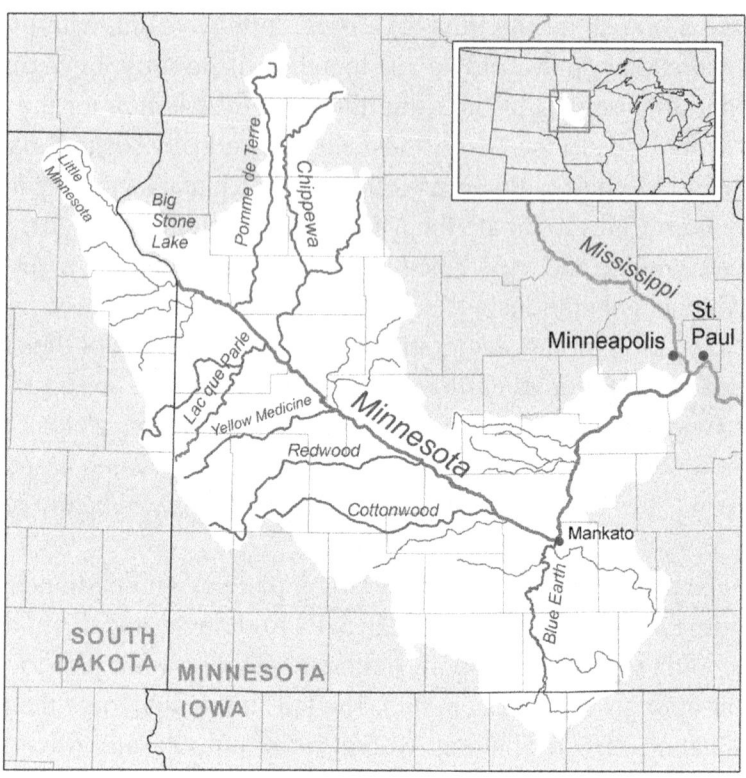

*Minnesota and Little Minnesota (bold) River System.
Map courtesy of KMusser/Images.*

Finally, entertain the fact that a few miles downstream from its source at Lake Itasca, the Mississippi flows into the west side of a lake, Bemidji, from which water finds a river outlet on the east side and eventually heads south to the Twin Cities. Similarly, water of the Little Minnesota River flows into the north end of Big Stone Lake and finds a river outlet at the south end where it is called the Minnesota River. Should we call the stretch of the Mississippi between Itasca and Lake Bemidji the Little Mississippi? Should the Little Minnesota be renamed Minnesota? Hmmmm.

So readers, now you have some new(?) bits of information to chew on. After I masticated and digested the facts, I wanted to rename the stretch of the Mississippi upstream of the Twin Cities as the Itasca River. On my new map, the name Mississippi replaces

Minnesota and Little Minnesota.

There are other possibilities. Maybe the Little Minnesota and Minnesota Rivers should retain their present identities and join the Itasca River at the Twin Cities to become the Mississippi? I invite you to get creative with friends and discuss possible name changes at your local chat-and-chew, over a cup of coffee and a slice of home-made apple pie.

Whatever any of us may feel about river names, I understand that an official change for labels of any part of the current Mississippi River is unlikely. Serial approval of local, then state, and finally federal agencies would be needed. Politics would surely intervene, especially because the interests of two states are involved.

Change can happen though. For example, the name for the part of today's Colorado River that is in fact within the state of Colorado was changed from Grand to Colorado in 1921, at the request of the state.

Stuff happens! So I hope South Dakotans, and the citizens of Veblen and Browns Valley in particular, will appreciate and spread the word about the fascinating history of lakes and rivers that have shaped much of their part of the Upper Midwest during the past few thousand years. If he could speak, I think the Browns Valley Man would have a lot to say on this topic. Ditto for my Grandpa Weeks. He was a wise and patient no-nonsense dirt farmer near Peever, South Dakota, who lived to love and understand his land and how it came to be.

CHANGING CLIMATE, THE KEELING CURVE, AND ME
Science in the Climate Change "Debate"

FOR ALL BUT the most avid head-in-the-sand deniers, Earth's climate is warming. Yes, there is a valid distinction between weather and climate, the latter being the average of the former over a long period — many centuries, or perhaps somewhat shorter periods if the rate of change is relatively rapid. As author Robert A. Heinlein aptly summarized the situation, "Climate is what you expect. Weather is what you get." So whereas no single storm, or weather averaged over only a year or two or three, is a valid indication of climate change, eventually slow-reacting temperature-dependent processes result in physical evidence of warming that is impossible to discount. People may argue in good faith about the time-related trend of near-surface temperatures measured as part of daily weather tracking, but when polar and other ice masses melt and sea level rises, it's because global climate is warming.

Mountain glaciers are in retreat. The Arctic and Antarctic ice sheets are measurably shrinking. For the first time in human history, a Northwest Passage is open for east to west Atlantic-Pacific navigation not dependent on the Panama Canal or Cape Horn. The Greenland icecap is shrinking and in so doing provides increasing vegetative evidence that this country's name perhaps is not such a terrible misnomer. Even extreme weather events, those short-term factoids that individually are not conclusive evidence of global warming, seem to be increasingly common in disrupting human life.

The Earth's atmosphere is a mixture of gaseous compounds whose proportions comprise a blanket that modulates the amount of sun's heat-in versus heat-out on a daily basis. Change in proportions alters the effectiveness of this blanket. Although it amounts to less than 1 percent of the atmosphere, carbon dioxide (CO_2) is a key constituent in the heat balance. More CO_2 results in less of the sun's heat escaping back to outer space on a daily basis. When continued, this effect results in climate warming.

Samples of Earth's atmosphere are trapped in ice sheets as the snows of winter storms become compacted into glacial ice. Drill cores of this ice contain bubbles that are representative of the atmosphere back through time. Chemical analyses of the bubbles indicate that atmospheric CO_2 has varied between 180 and 280 ppm (parts per million) during the past many millennia. Concomitantly, climate has varied. For example, glaciers have come and gone during this time window of Earth's history.

Today the concentration of CO_2 in the atmosphere is 400 ppm, a much higher value than any trapped in the ice cores. Incontrovertible evidence of the rise to this value since the mid twentieth century comes from the measurements of a simple experiment that began in 1958 at a weather observatory at ten-thousand-feet elevation on the north slope of Mauna Loa Volcano, Hawaii. The graphical plot of CO_2 versus time at Mauna Loa is called the Keeling Curve, named for Charles Keeling, who initiated the collection of data there. Many measurements have been made each year, often daily or even more frequently.

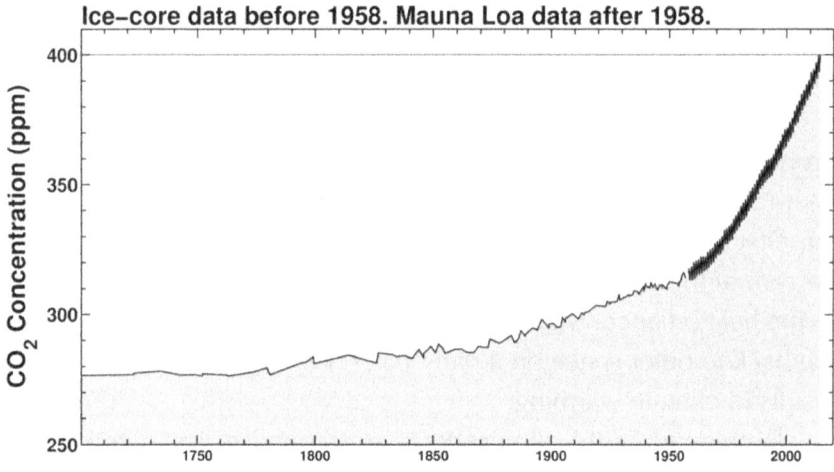

Carbon dioxide in Earth's atmosphere since 1700 CE (or AD 1700, if you prefer). A noticeable increase begins about mid-nineteenth century, the time when human population was rapidly increasing, as was the burning of fossil carbon-based fuels. Figure courtesy of Scripps Institution of Oceanography.

Keeling chose this location in the middle of the Pacific Ocean in order to be far from any industrial source of CO_2. The only "unwanted" point source might be the volcano itself. Volcanoes emit CO_2 as magma rises close to and eventually appears at the surface where this gas, dissolved in magma, can escape into the atmosphere. Mauna Loa is an active volcano that has had many historic eruptions, including one in 1984 during the period of measurements that comprise the Keeling curve. Among other features, the shape of the Keeling curve across 1984 indicates that volcano CO_2 did not "contaminate" the general atmospheric value. If a volcanic effect had occurred, the overall regular shape of the plot would have been distorted during the time of the eruption.

An annual up-and-down sawtooth pattern of the Keeling Curve results from slight CO_2 intake by land plants during summer growth, followed by release of that CO_2 during plant dormancy, death, and decay in winter.

The overall first-order trend is an increase of CO_2 with the passage of time. This means the insulating efficacy of the atmospheric blanket simultaneously increases with time. The source of the continuing addition of CO_2 derives mostly from an increase in combustion of carbon-based fuels as human population grows.

Perhaps more importantly, in terms of an escalating impact on Earth's climate, the discerning eye also sees that the long-term Keeling trend is not linear. The upward steepening slope indicates that the *rate* at which CO_2 is increasing in the atmosphere is also increasing with time. More and more fuel-consuming humans means more and more fuel burned. If this situation persists, the atmosphere is on a "runaway" path to concentrations of CO_2 much higher than 400 ppm. People who don't understand this situation and/or refuse to accept the analytical data present no plausible alternative explanation.

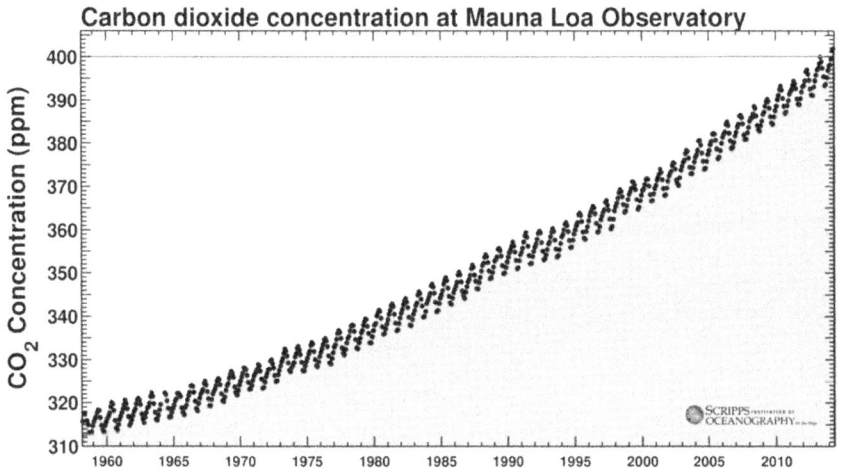

Figure courtesy of Scripps Institution of Oceanography.

Climate-warming deniers would likely consider funds spent for a project such as Keeling's as wasted resources. Yet without frequent repeated measurements over a period of decades, the graphically incontrovertible evidence of continuous increase, and rate of increase of CO_2 in the atmosphere might not exist.

I visited the Mauna Loa Observatory in 1970 and again in 1971. I was a member of a team of geologists who visited the summit of Mauna Loa annually to make measurements that track the potential for impending eruption of the volcano. We spent the first night of our ascents at the Observatory to help acclimate our bodies to the next day's summit elevation of nearly fourteen thousand feet.

On both visits, a hand-drawn plot of those first few years of CO_2 measurements was tacked to the observatory wall — the very beginnings of today's fifty-six-year record. I had no idea that I was looking at the initial stage of what would eventually become a world-famous graph.

I invite readers to cover the Keeling Curve beyond the year 1971, and then ask yourselves if you could have anticipated what the overall shape would be by 2014. Even rigorous mathematical curve fitting and projection would have yielded only a broad range of possibilities at best. Science advances by repeated rigorous testing. Sometimes a science experiment advances slowly, in small incremental steps. An important message carried by the Keeling Curve is to not abandon the journey before the direction of the path is well defined. Or, as my Stanford professor and hero Si Muller might say, *Don't take short cuts if you want to accurately portray your scientific research.*

THAT DAMMED COLORADO RIVER!!

AIRHEAD ARMCHAIR PHILOSOPHERS have been known to pontificate that water flows downhill, an obvious yet important generalization. When a volcano erupts, the ground-hugging products (be they lava flows or turbulent flows of fragmental debris) also move downhill, powered by the same force that moves flowing water ... gravity. Should such volcanic stuff encounter and come to rest in the valley of an active river, a dam is likely to be instantaneously constructed. The new upstream reservoir immediately begins to fill. And the story that unfolds beyond then depends on a variety of factors related to the size and strength of the new dam and the rate at which water is added to the reservoir.

There must have been hundreds or thousands or even many many more such occurrences in planet Earth's long volcanic history. Even historical examples are fairly common. I had a professional experience with one in 1982 at El Chichon Volcano in Chiapas, Mexico. Lessons learned help guide those whose concern is recognizing natural hazards and making plans for their mitigation.

Counting Hoover Dam near Boulder City, Nevada, and Glen Canyon Dam near Page, Arizona, as bounding bookends, twenty other dams have been built along the intervening path of the Colorado River. Actually, the total number of these constructions is uncertain; it may be a bit more or less than twenty. But what is certain is that only Hoover and Glen Canyon are creations of mankind. The other dams are the products of basalt lava flows erupted from scores of river-flanking volcanoes. A few landslide-created dams add to an overall total, but the volcanic constructs are the focus here.

Deists might credit Hawaii's Pele, or whatever their favorite volcano goddess/god figure may be, for these lava eruptions. As a volcanologist who cut his professional teeth, to say nothing about actually cutting a variety of his flesh-covered body parts while studying the hot, sharp, and glassy basalt lavas of Kilauea Volcano where Pele currently resides, I can imagine that she might have repeatedly vacationed on the mainland and conjured up eruptions there to disrupt the smooth uninterrupted flow of water along what would eventually be named the Colorado River of North America once humans of European stock appeared on the scene.

Yet, as a research scientist I realize that a naturally hot, roiling, and unstable rocky mantle a few miles beneath the Uinkaret Plateau of the Colorado River corridor partly melted into basalt magma that cork-like buoyed upward to the surface, time after time, where it fed lava flows that spilled into the canyon to build dams. Pele's purported supernatural talents are unnecessary. Earth's internal heat drove the process and is capable of doing so again and again.

The vents for most of the dam-building volcanoes are located on and a bit beyond the north rim of the canyon. A couple sit atop the south rim. All are sandwiched between the north/south-trending Toroweap and Whitmore Canyon Faults. Each is what geologists call a basalt cinder (or scoria) cone volcano, which typically erupts fluidal lava flows over a period of a few years, while building a cone-shaped pile of cinders (scoria) at the vent.

View to the NNE across the canyon of the Colorado River where eruptions created lava dams. The thin dark-colored rocks are basalt lava flows draped over a thick succession of horizontal sedimentary formations. The cinder cone on the north canyon rim is Vulcan's Throne.

During his exploration of the Grand Canyon in 1869, John Wesley Powell was the first scientist to visit and later publish descriptions of the remnants of nature's lava dams across the Colorado River. Many geologists have since supplemented Powell's observations, with the benefit of ever-improving analytical techniques that help add information about when each dam formed, its probable height, its life span, and the current status of dismemberment by erosion. As of 2014, the accumulated data suggest that at least seventeen eruptions created dams at various times between eight hundred fifty thousand and a hundred thousand years ago.

Suggest is an important qualifying word in the previous sentence. Documentation of the formation of each dam and its current near-total erosional destruction derives from mere bits and pieces left behind. Some lava-dam remnants are in their original positions, attached at various heights on the canyon walls. Other dam fragments are now downstream gravel and boulder deposits. Reconstructing the life story of a lava dam from such evidence is complicated.

For example, lava flow remnants attached to opposite canyon walls at the same elevation are not necessarily parts of what was originally a single level lava dam. All dam remnants are basalt, and basalt is quite homogeneous in appearance and chemical composition. However, some minor chemical constituents may vary from flow to flow, providing a possible tool to help determine whether or not those two side-wall bits are part and parcel of a single flow.

View to the NNE. Stream-like ribbons of black are basalt lava flows, several of which spilled into Whitmore Canyon on the left as they moved toward, and some into the Grand Canyon. Colorado River is visible in the lower right. The Vulcan's Throne area is upstream from here.

Even with exact matches in rock chemistry, however, two flow remnants attached to opposite canyon walls at the same elevation may differ in their eruption age. The time of eruption in years before the present is recorded in a rock by radioactive constituents that begin their time-keeping as soon as lava solidifies and thus begins to trap the products of their radioactive decay. More time means more decay, which occurs at a known rate. The uncertainty attached to a calculated age can be thousands or even tens of thousands of years. Different ages beyond uncertainty limits of so-called radiometric ages indicate lava flows of different eruptions.

Lacking the somewhat expensive and time-consuming determination of radiometric age, even something as simple as determining relative ages of two lava flow remnants in stacked contact with each other can contradict geology's fundamental "Law of Superposition." *In a layered sequence of rock formations that have not been overturned, the age of separate layers decreases successively upward.* In their Grand Canyon setting, however, a lava remnant that abuts against a wall can be directly underlain by a younger remnant that flowed into place once most of the original older and higher lava dam had been eroded away. Sigh!!

The difficult job for the geologist is to critically analyze such a hodge-podge of evidence, knowing that he/she is confronted with a challenging exercise analogous to accurately creating the cover image of a picture puzzle when so many of the individual pieces are missing. It's today's state-of-the-art reconstruction within such uncertainties that suggests nearly twenty lava dams were created across the Colorado River in the Grand Canyon since eight hundred fifty thousand years ago.

"So what?" a random lay reader might opine. "I'm not a geologist, but I pretty much grasp the technical stuff and understand the pitfalls in trying to uncover the details of the history of forming those lava dams. Still, why should I care about exactly how many times it happened? Especially since you geologists say the last dam is a hundred thousand years old! What's that ancient history got to do with my life or those of foreseeable generations?"

I caution that yes, the youngest dam formed about then. But there's no scientific justification to call it the *last* (the doubter's word). It's just the most recent.

Consider this fact. The most recent eruption in the group of volcanoes that created all the dams took place about nine hundred years ago. People were there watching the fireworks. Blobs of the lava splattered down on some of their pottery. The heat and noise might have sent them fleeing in fear. The scene of Earth opening to spew out molten rock must have been a mind-bending experience. It likely gave rise to new tales of folklore.

That eruption didn't last long enough to feed a lava flow all the way to and into the canyon. But given the overall record of eruptions in the area, any thinking geologist would be beyond foolish to predict that there will be no future eruption that could create a lava dam. If nearby seismometers ever start shaking from a tremor that typically reflects magma working its way upward, the next eruption may be imminent. Maybe it will spill into the canyon.

A tall new lava dam with a large full upstream reservoir that emptied quickly, as many of the older ones appear to have done, could be devastating to downstream infrastructure and population centers. For an extreme case, imagine the possibility that a wall of water takes out Hoover Dam as it surges downstream.

The threat of breaching both Glen Canyon and Hoover dams occurred in 1983, without the help of a volcano. That spring, snow melt and rain of a particularly wet season filled Lake Powell to above the level of overflow spillways at Glen Canyon dam. By dam-construction design, overflow was channeled into forty-one-foot-diameter concrete-lined tunnels through bedrock on each side of the dam. This was the first time these tunnels had been put to use. Faulty design triggered a process called cavitation (creation of low-pressure air pockets that are sources of damaging shock waves when they collapse), which destroyed large sections of the concrete walls and permitted the erosion of the much softer sedimentary rocks behind the concrete. Had the rise of water in Lake Powell not serendipitously stopped before the degree of cavitation destruction became critical, the lake would likely have quickly drained, sending a downstream flow that might have caused Hoover to fail, or at least release unplanned and uncontrolled volumes of water. The potential havoc wreaked is limited only by one's imagination.

Food for thought: When Hoover and Glen Canyon dams were built (1931–36 and 1956–63), the age of the youngest eruption within the field of volcanoes that created lava dams in the Grand Canyon was not known. That only came to light about 2005. I wonder if the construction and design of those dams would have been modified if a significantly higher probability of a new lava dam within, say, a few hundred years had been known.

CPSIA information can be obtained
at www.ICGtesting.com
Printed in the USA
FSOW03n0712081015
11952FS

Just in Case You Were W...

Wendell A. "Duff" Duffield was ... Midwest family-farm country. At age 15, ... w England, where he graduated fr... y in 195... He next earned a BA at Carleton ... PhD from Stanford University (1967) ... e decade he studied volcanoes for the U.S. ... 97, he "retired" to become an Adjunct ... ern Arizona University, Flagstaff. In 2015, Duff and his wife, Anne, moved to Greenbank, Washington, where they garden, read, write, and age.

Have you ever wondered what a serious research scientist writes during "spare" moments? These folks are not all one-track-mind nerds. This book invites you to explore the life path of a small-town Upper Midwest farm boy who unexpectedly found himself on a heady track of education that produced a PhD-toting geologist devoted to learning about volcanoes. Early on in this career, the core joy of publishing results of his fiery research projects branched into writing essays on a variety of other topics. A few pieces appeared in "gray literature" along the way. This book compiles several of these miscellaneous writings, including discussions of organized religion, global warming, piloting small aircraft, family dynamics, quirks along a path of higher education, earthy humor, and the role of serendipity in all phases of life. All readers will identify with one or more of these topics. Some folks may even become inspired to sit at a keyboard and enter their own life tales before memory fades beyond accurate recall.

Kalynn Gunderson is an illustrator and story teller living in Tucson, Arizona. She studied art at the University of Arizona and is freshly embarking on her artistic career. When she isn't painting she enjoys designing characters and writing stories about them.

BIOGRAPHY & AUTOBIOGRAPHY / Personal Memoirs

ISBN 978-1-4787-6385-7

OutskirtsPress.com

U.S. $12.95